A FUNNY THING HAPPENED ON THE WAY TO SAN DIEGO...

An Introduction by Paul Castiglia

It was one of those moments of spontaneous inspiration. In the middle of an editorial meeting like any other, there was one nagging piece of unfinished business. Richard Goldwater, President and Co-Publisher, and Michael Silberkleit, Chairman and Co-Publisher, posed the question: "What can we do to propel Archie and his friends into the collective consciousness as never before?" Fred Mausser, VP of Sales, suggested we create an epic **"cross-over"** storyline within **four** Archie titles. But what would the "hook" be? Naturally, we couldn't have one of our squeaky-clean teens perish, but with visions of "Death of Superman" flying through my head, I searched my Archie-data-filled cranium for the one idea that would be just as exciting. It hit me like Cupid's arrow. I blurted out, "What if Betty and Veronica had a **once-and-for-all** competition for Archie's affections?" Questions abounded: How would we stage it? What would the outcome be? From there, credit must go to ace writers Bill Golliher and Dan Parent and Managing Editor Victor Gorelick, whose abundance of creativity fleshed out the initial concept. The room exploded with enthusiasm, and I started to daydream about **national** attention for this story.

About eight months later, the first installment was just weeks away from publication. Retailers assured me that Archie Comics had a "hot" commodity in its hands — something the country at large should know about. I figured that even if **one** newspaper had reported the news, we will have succeeded. Initiating my first media blitz with great anxiety, I took on the task of compiling press materials while preparing for the biggest convention of the year — the San Diego ComicCon. Would all this effort pay off? Would I be able to get the word out **and** make it to the convention?

August 4th, **at the convention,** I sat down to breakfast with my comrades. We were pleasantly surprised to find the "Archie News" prominently displayed in **USA Today.** The timing couldn't have been better! All day excited fans stopped by our booth, asking if it was really true, and begging us to tell them who Archie would pick. If this was any indication, we were in for a lot of attention! And attention we got, as newspapers across the US and Canada chronicled the story of **Archie's Love Showdown** — they were as concerned with the love lives of Riverdale's teens as they were with the national debt! Meanwhile, on countless radio and TV shows, grown men and women shamelessly debated the merits of who would make a better choice — Betty or Veronica? Needless to say, comic book retailers had a lot to smile about as fans **of all ages** relentlessly pursued this most sought-after saga!

Why has this story captured the public's imagination? The answer is easy. Just as daytime soap opera fans get caught up in the lives of their fictional characters (often to the point where they consider them real people, so too do Archie fans respond to these classic and timely youngsters! There was no way they were going to miss **this** chapter of the entertainment world's most famous teens!

To date, millions have heard of the **apparent demise** of Archie Comics' love triangle, so popular demand dictates we let everyone re-live Archie Andrews' pitfalls of young romance. For those who may be experiencing this milestone series for the first time, you can now enjoy all of the chapters in one handsome volume. Either way, it just goes to show you: you **can** have your "Kate and Edith too" — but not without complications!

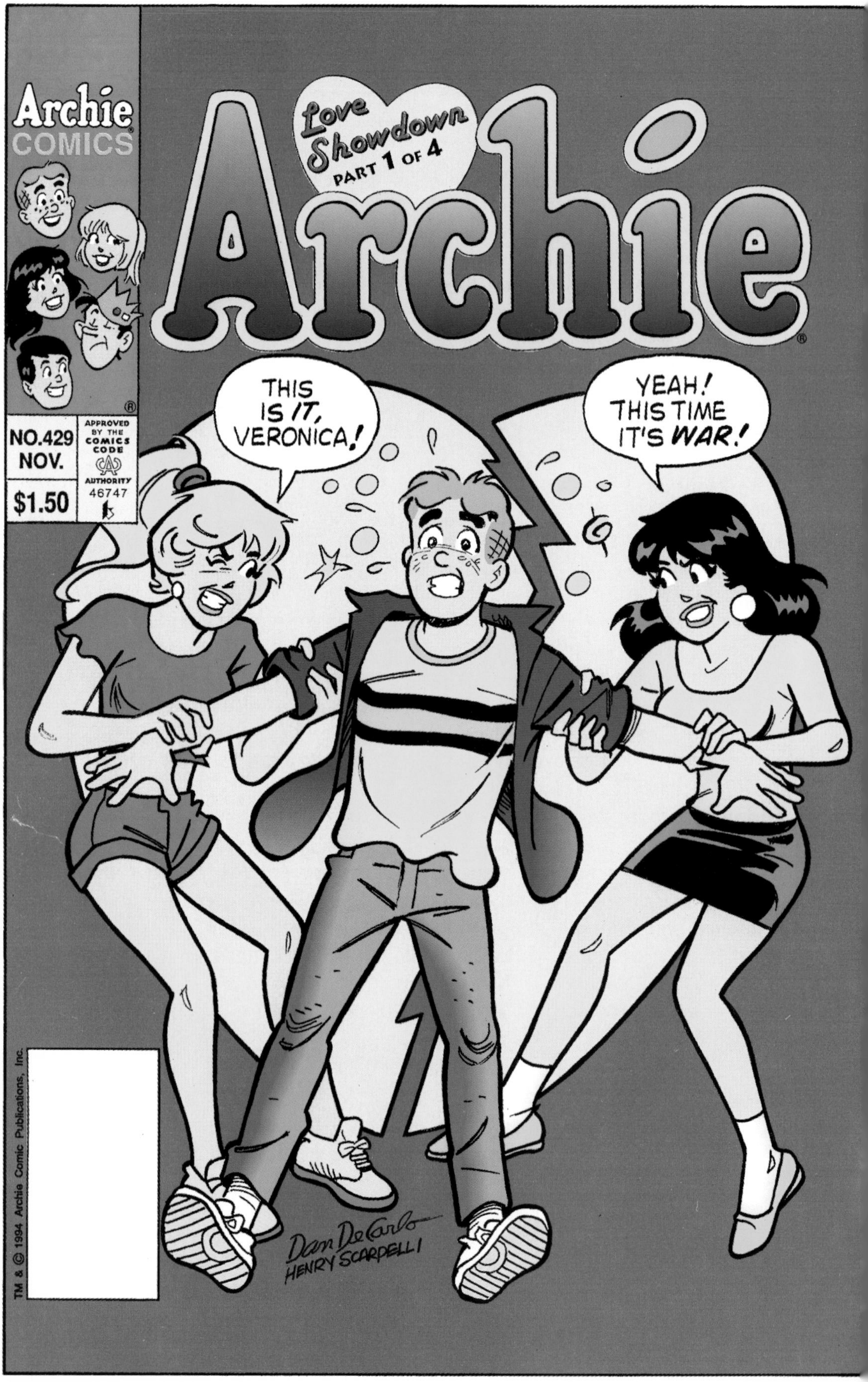
Archie COMICS
Love Showdown PART 1 OF 4
Archie
NO.429 NOV.
$1.50
APPROVED BY THE COMICS CODE AUTHORITY
46747
THIS IS IT, VERONICA!
YEAH! THIS TIME IT'S WAR!
Dan DeCarlo
HENRY SCARPELLI
TM & © 1994 Archie Comic Publications, Inc.

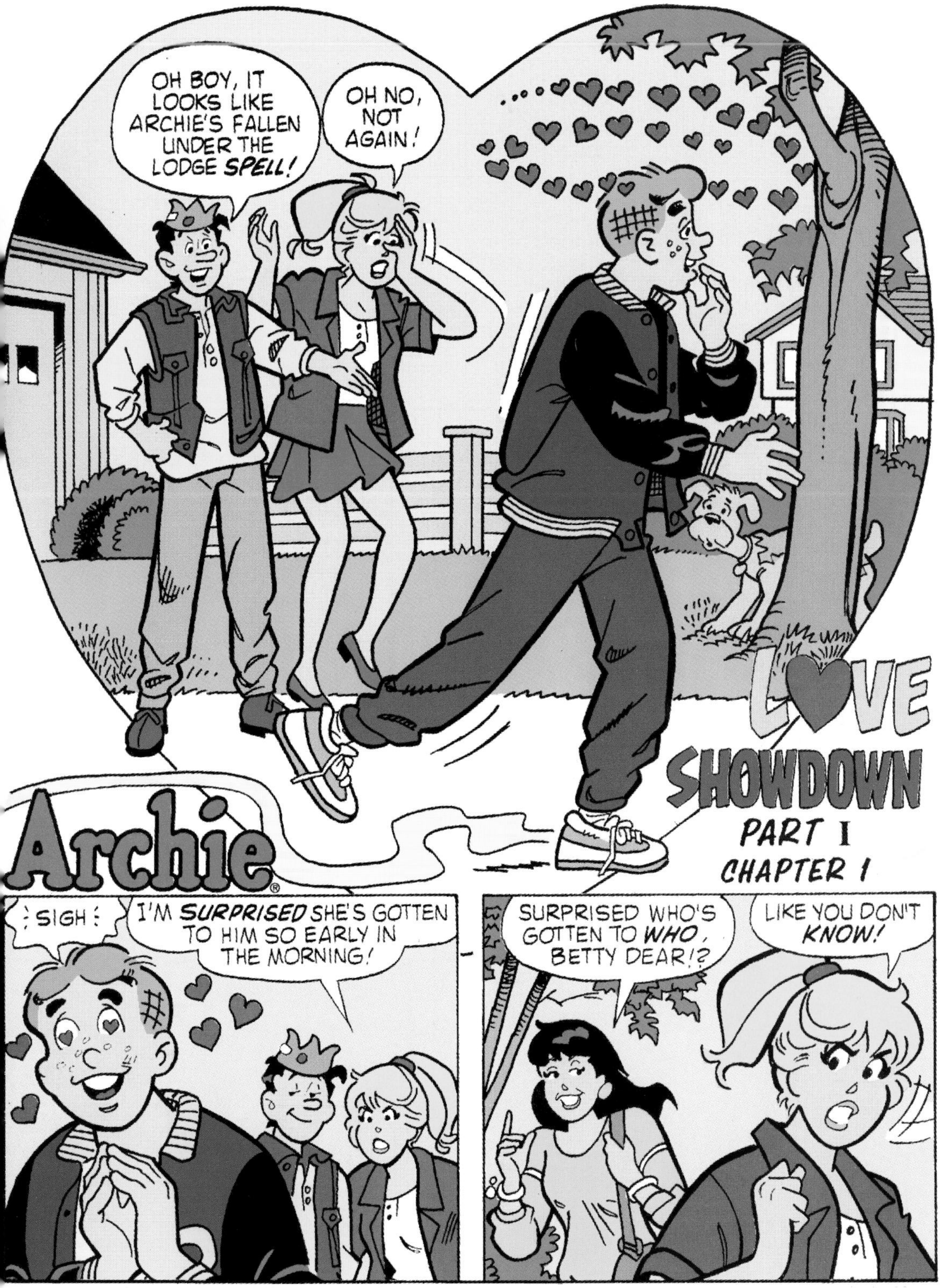
OH BOY, IT LOOKS LIKE ARCHIE'S FALLEN UNDER THE LODGE SPELL!
OH NO, NOT AGAIN!
LOVE SHOWDOWN
PART I
CHAPTER 1
Archie
SIGH
I'M SURPRISED SHE'S GOTTEN TO HIM SO EARLY IN THE MORNING!
SURPRISED WHO'S GOTTEN TO WHO, BETTY DEAR!?
LIKE YOU DON'T KNOW!

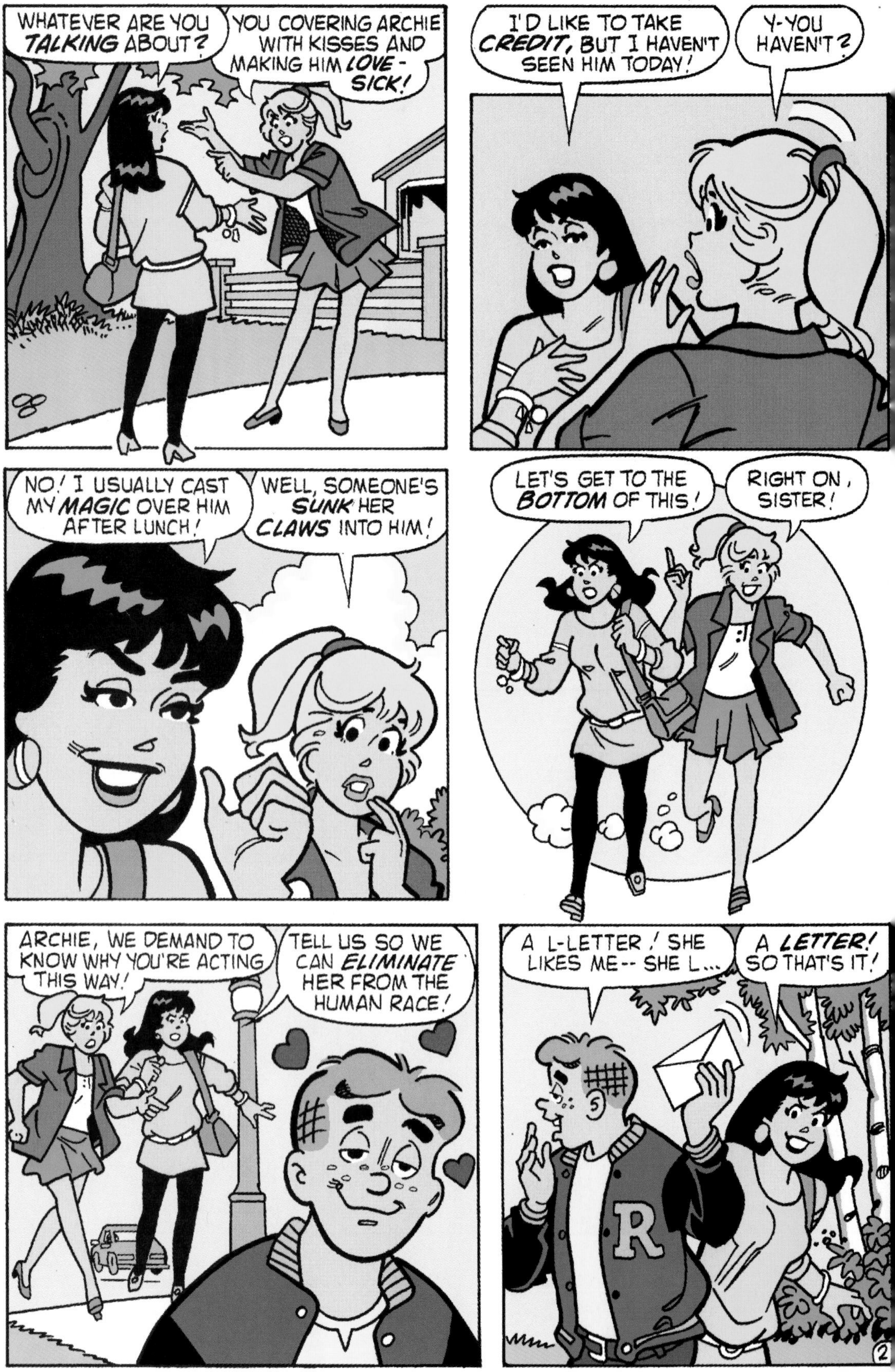

WHATEVER ARE YOU TALKING ABOUT?
YOU COVERING ARCHIE WITH KISSES AND MAKING HIM LOVE-SICK!
I'D LIKE TO TAKE CREDIT, BUT I HAVEN'T SEEN HIM TODAY!
Y-YOU HAVEN'T?
NO! I USUALLY CAST MY MAGIC OVER HIM AFTER LUNCH!
WELL, SOMEONE'S SUNK HER CLAWS INTO HIM!
LET'S GET TO THE BOTTOM OF THIS!
RIGHT ON, SISTER!
ARCHIE, WE DEMAND TO KNOW WHY YOU'RE ACTING THIS WAY!
TELL US SO WE CAN ELIMINATE HER FROM THE HUMAN RACE!
A L-LETTER! SHE LIKES ME-- SHE L...
A LETTER! SO THAT'S IT!
2

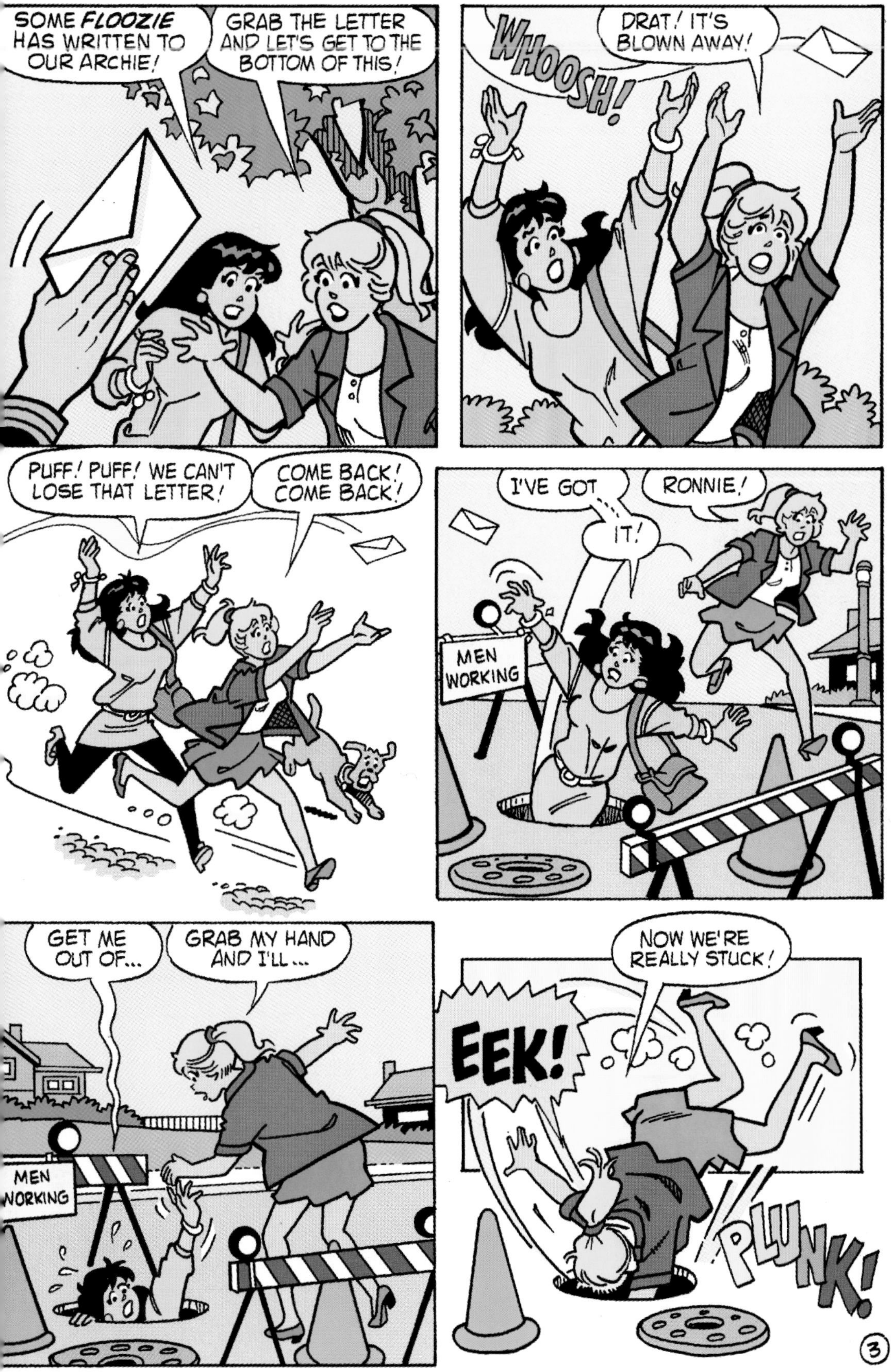
SOME FLOOZIE HAS WRITTEN TO OUR ARCHIE!
GRAB THE LETTER AND LET'S GET TO THE BOTTOM OF THIS!
WHOOSH!
DRAT! IT'S BLOWN AWAY!
PUFF! PUFF! WE CAN'T LOSE THAT LETTER!
COME BACK! COME BACK!
I'VE GOT
IT!
RONNIE!
MEN WORKING
GET ME OUT OF...
GRAB MY HAND AND I'LL...
MEN WORKING
NOW WE'RE REALLY STUCK!
EEK!
PLUNK!

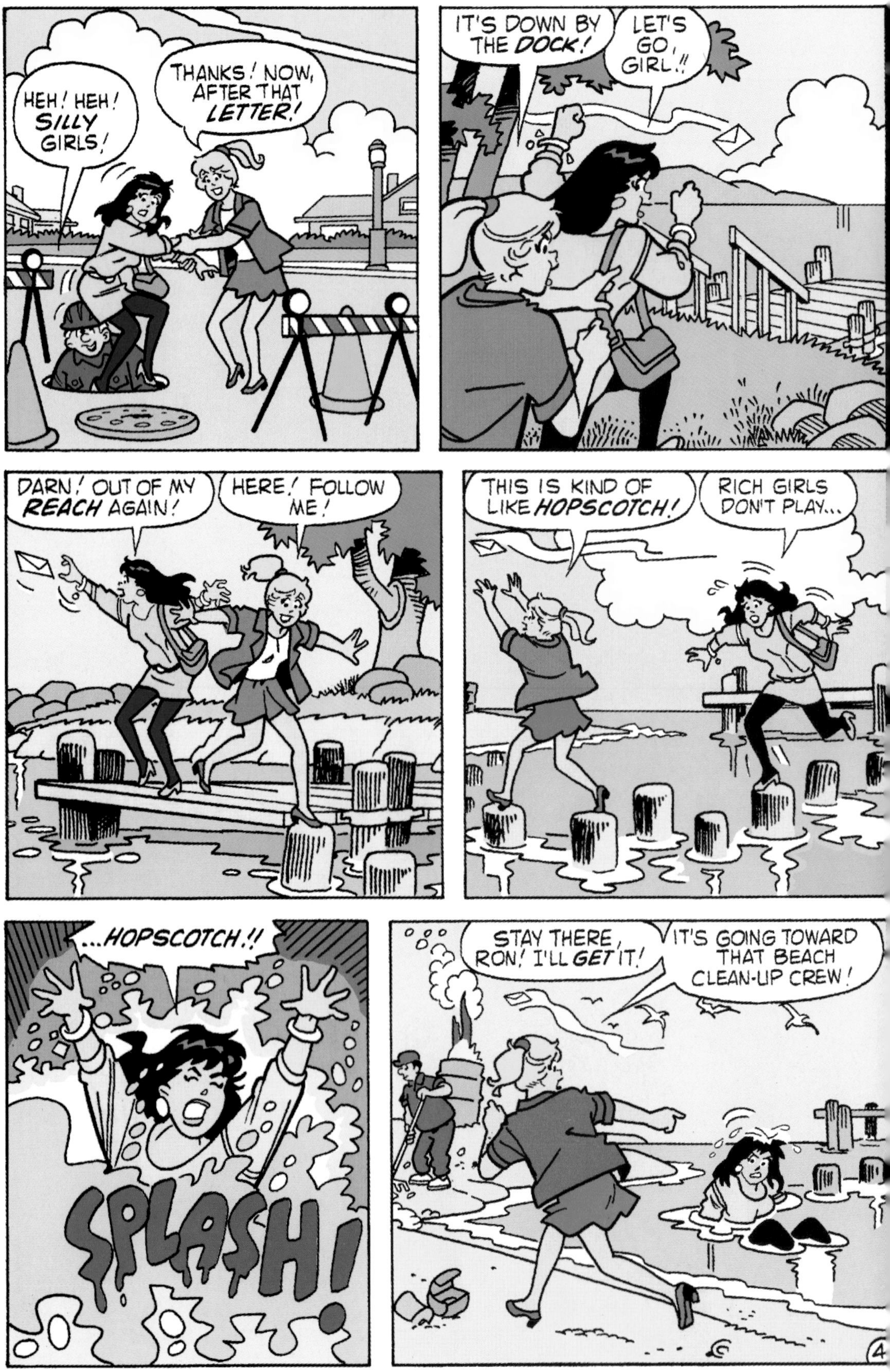

HEH! HEH! SILLY GIRLS!
THANKS! NOW, AFTER THAT LETTER!
IT'S DOWN BY THE DOCK!
LET'S GO, GIRL!!
DARN! OUT OF MY REACH AGAIN!
HERE! FOLLOW ME!
THIS IS KIND OF LIKE HOPSCOTCH!
RICH GIRLS DON'T PLAY...
...HOPSCOTCH!!
SPLASH!
STAY THERE, RON! I'LL GET IT!
IT'S GOING TOWARD THAT BEACH CLEAN-UP CREW!
4

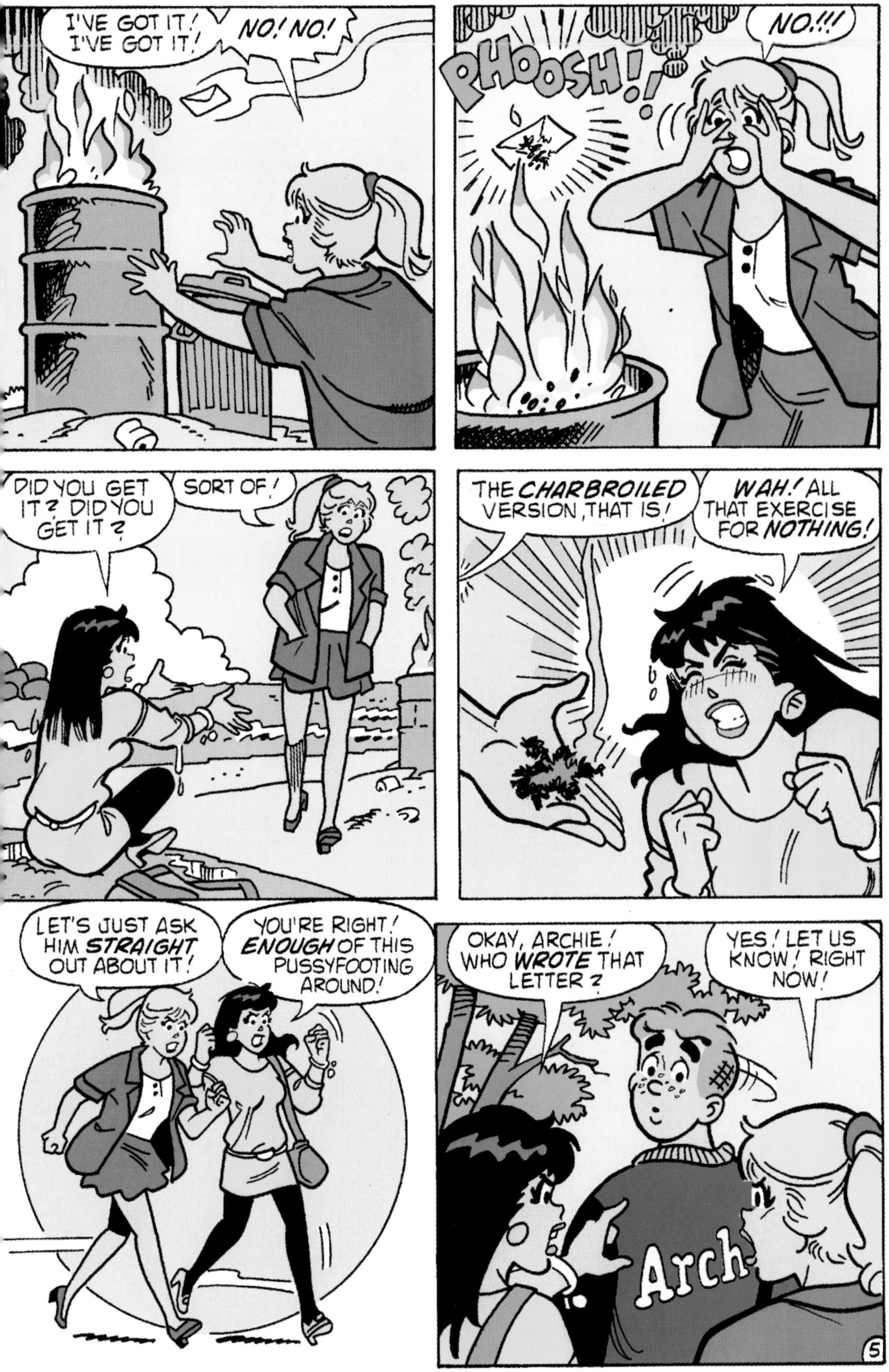
I'VE GOT IT! I'VE GOT IT!
NO! NO!
PHOOSH!!
NO!!!
DID YOU GET IT? DID YOU GET IT?
SORT OF!
THE CHARBROILED VERSION, THAT IS!
WAH! ALL THAT EXERCISE FOR NOTHING!
LET'S JUST ASK HIM STRAIGHT OUT ABOUT IT!
YOU'RE RIGHT! ENOUGH OF THIS PUSSYFOOTING AROUND!
OKAY, ARCHIE! WHO WROTE THAT LETTER?
YES! LET US KNOW! RIGHT NOW!
Arch
5

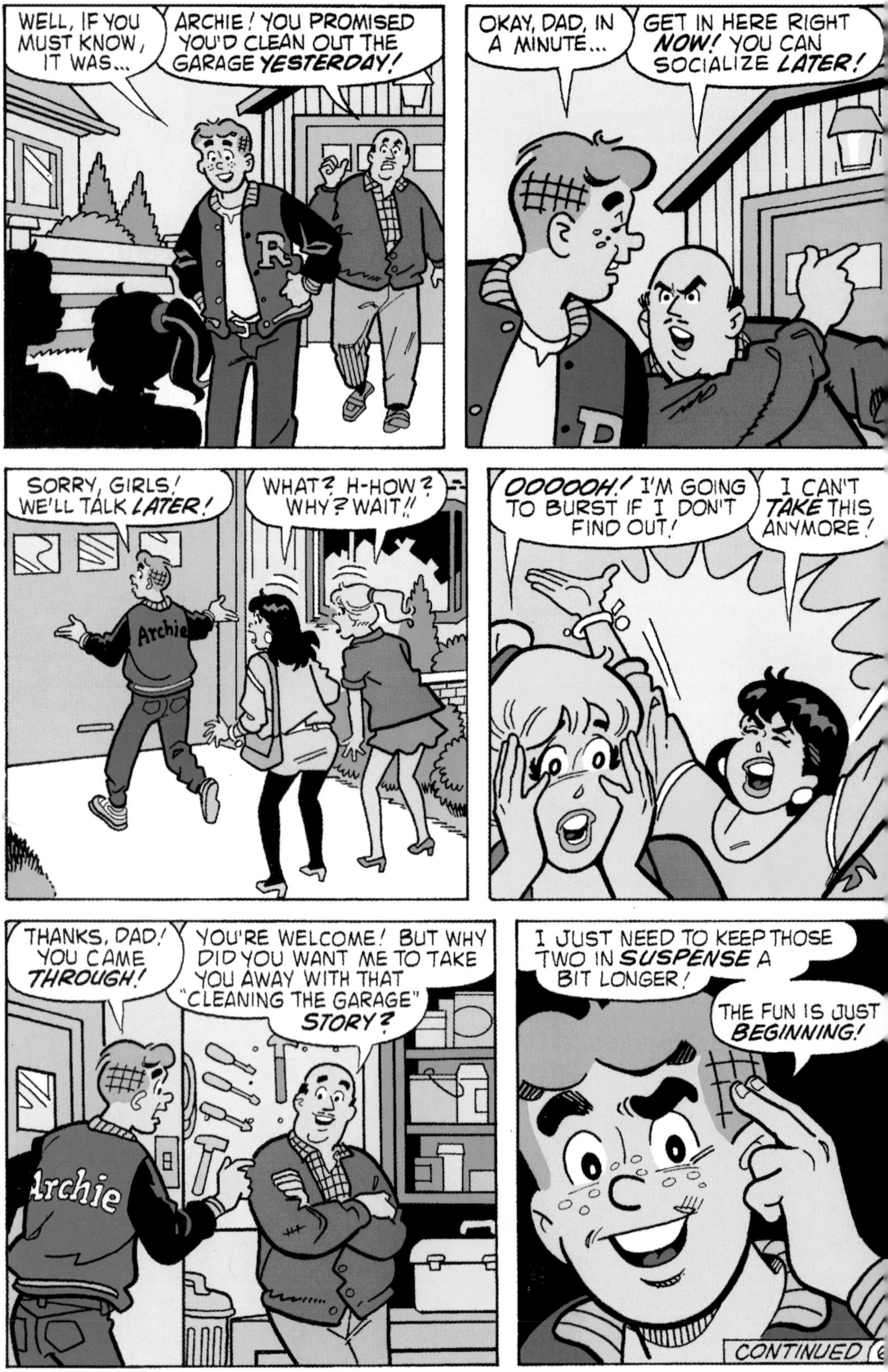
WELL, IF YOU MUST KNOW, IT WAS...
ARCHIE! YOU PROMISED YOU'D CLEAN OUT THE GARAGE YESTERDAY!
OKAY, DAD, IN A MINUTE...
GET IN HERE RIGHT NOW! YOU CAN SOCIALIZE LATER!
SORRY, GIRLS! WE'LL TALK LATER!
WHAT? H-HOW? WHY? WAIT!!
OOOOOOH! I'M GOING TO BURST IF I DON'T FIND OUT!
I CAN'T TAKE THIS ANYMORE!
THANKS, DAD! YOU CAME THROUGH!
YOU'RE WELCOME! BUT WHY DID YOU WANT ME TO TAKE YOU AWAY WITH THAT "CLEANING THE GARAGE" STORY?
I JUST NEED TO KEEP THOSE TWO IN SUSPENSE A BIT LONGER!
THE FUN IS JUST BEGINNING!
CONTINUED

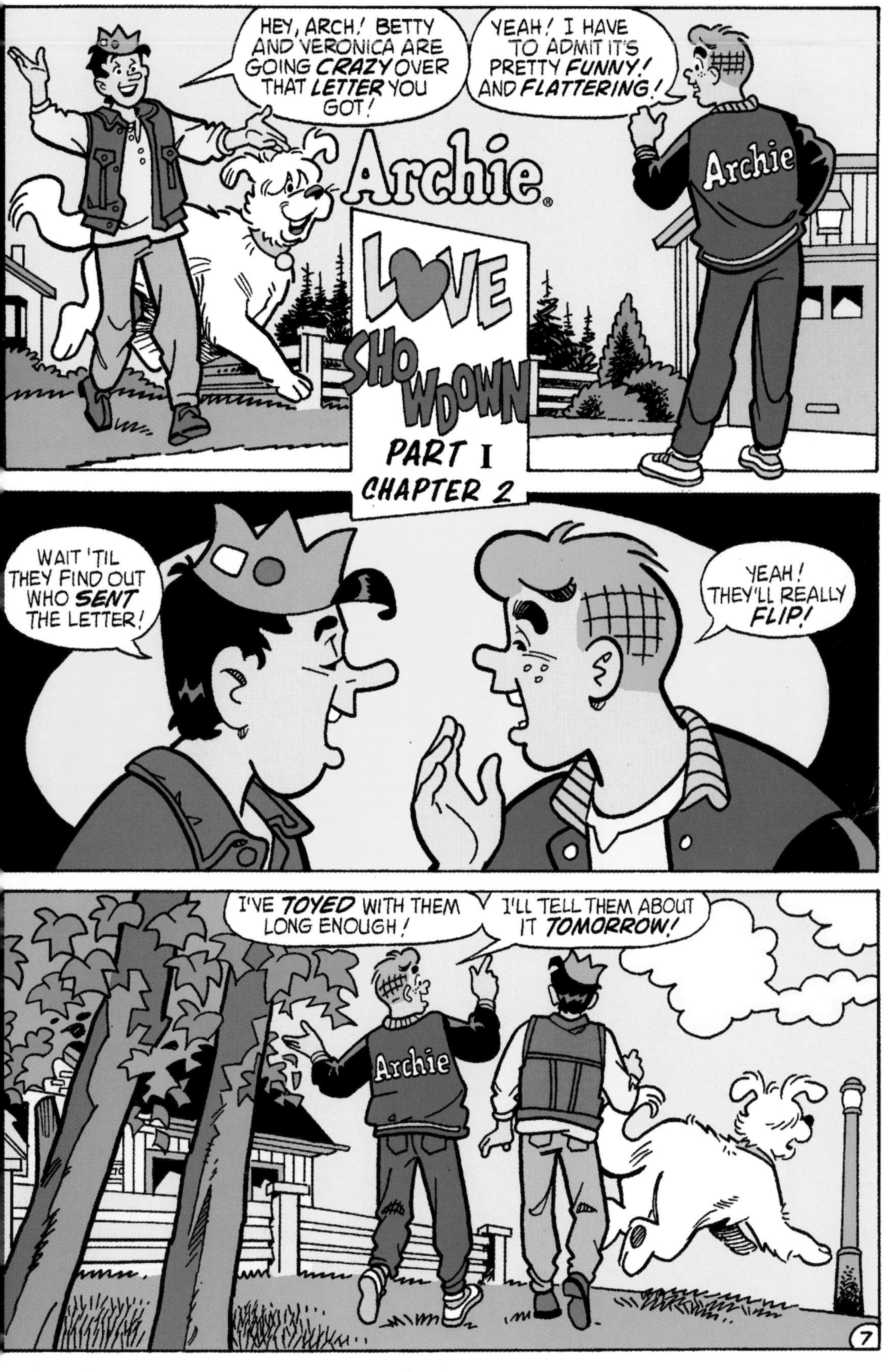
HEY, ARCH! BETTY AND VERONICA ARE GOING CRAZY OVER THAT LETTER YOU GOT!
YEAH! I HAVE TO ADMIT IT'S PRETTY FUNNY! AND FLATTERING!
Archie
LOVE SHOWDOWN
PART I
CHAPTER 2
Archie
WAIT 'TIL THEY FIND OUT WHO SENT THE LETTER!
YEAH! THEY'LL REALLY FLIP!
I'VE TOYED WITH THEM LONG ENOUGH!
I'LL TELL THEM ABOUT IT TOMORROW!
Archie
7

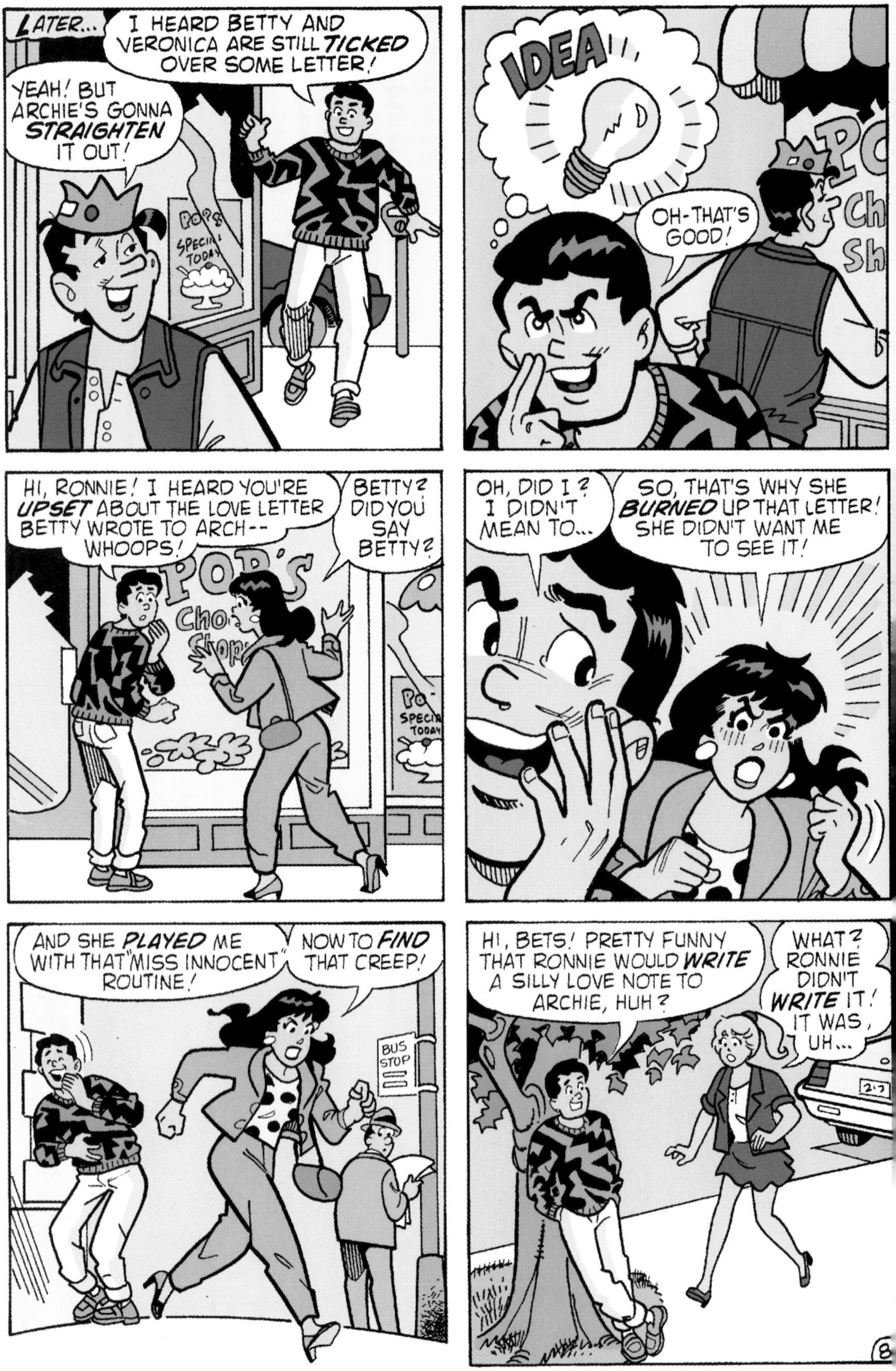
LATER...
I HEARD BETTY AND VERONICA ARE STILL TICKED OVER SOME LETTER!
YEAH! BUT ARCHIE'S GONNA STRAIGHTEN IT OUT!
POP'S SPECIAL TODAY
IDEA
OH-THAT'S GOOD!
HI, RONNIE! I HEARD YOU'RE UPSET ABOUT THE LOVE LETTER BETTY WROTE TO ARCH-- WHOOPS!
BETTY? DID YOU SAY BETTY?
OH, DID I? I DIDN'T MEAN TO...
SO, THAT'S WHY SHE BURNED UP THAT LETTER! SHE DIDN'T WANT ME TO SEE IT!
AND SHE PLAYED ME WITH THAT "MISS INNOCENT" ROUTINE!
NOW TO FIND THAT CREEP!
BUS STOP
HI, BETS! PRETTY FUNNY THAT RONNIE WOULD WRITE A SILLY LOVE NOTE TO ARCHIE, HUH?
WHAT? RONNIE DIDN'T WRITE IT! IT WAS, UH...

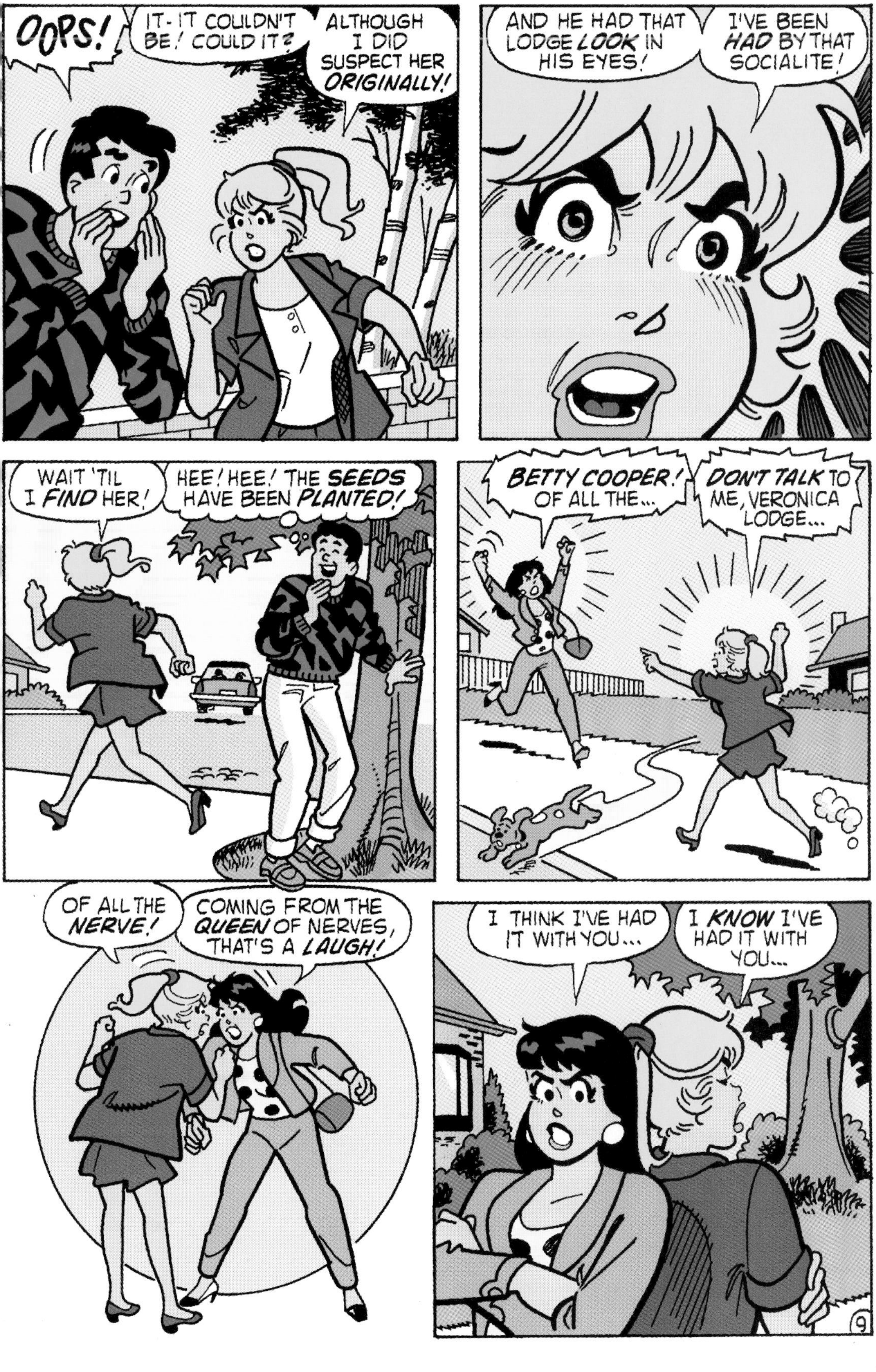

OOPS!
IT- IT COULDN'T BE! COULD IT?
ALTHOUGH I DID SUSPECT HER ORIGINALLY!
AND HE HAD THAT LODGE LOOK IN HIS EYES!
I'VE BEEN HAD BY THAT SOCIALITE!
WAIT 'TIL I FIND HER!
HEE! HEE! THE SEEDS HAVE BEEN PLANTED!
BETTY COOPER! OF ALL THE...
DON'T TALK TO ME, VERONICA LODGE...
OF ALL THE NERVE!
COMING FROM THE QUEEN OF NERVES, THAT'S A LAUGH!
I THINK I'VE HAD IT WITH YOU...
I KNOW I'VE HAD IT WITH YOU...
9

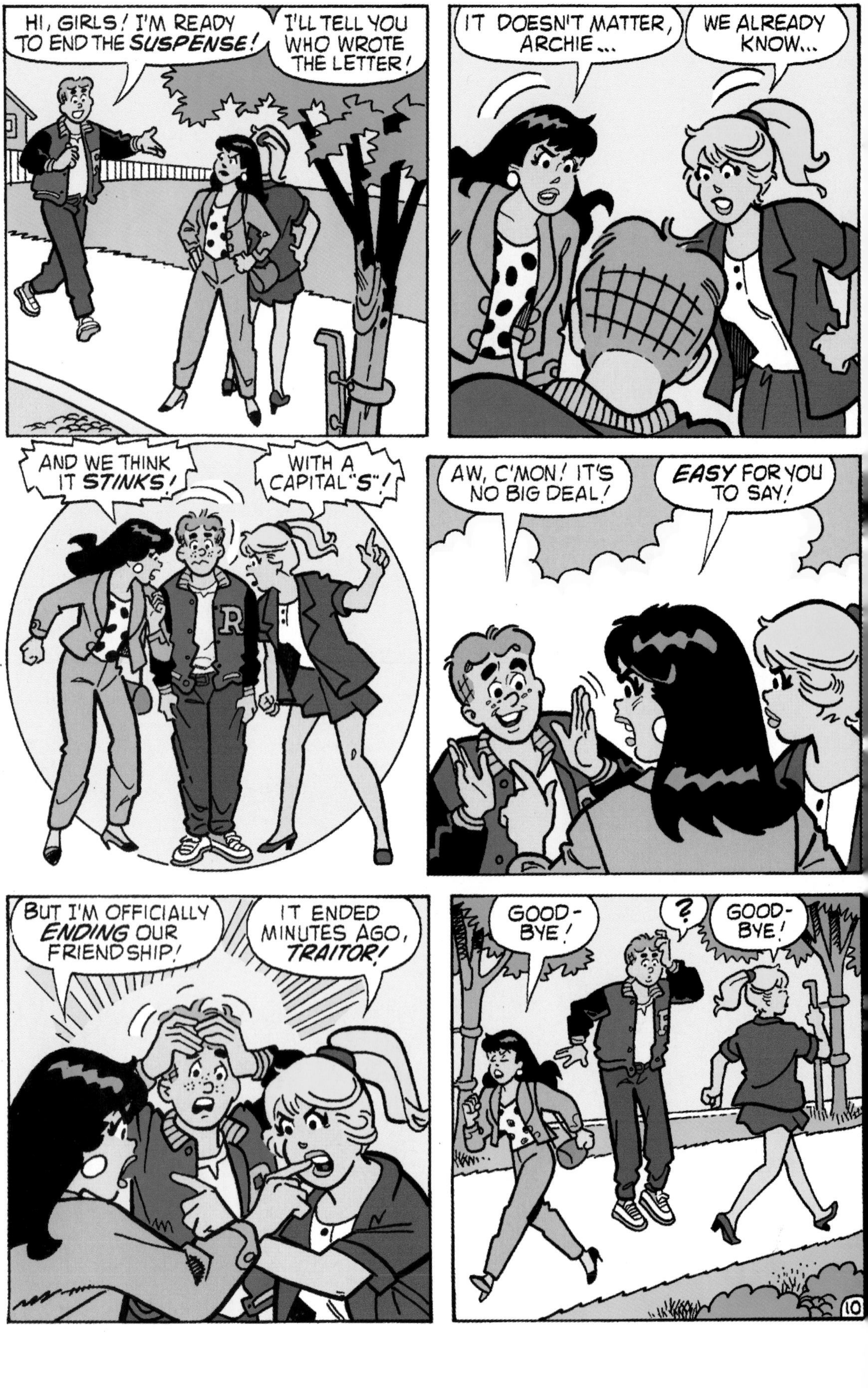
HI, GIRLS! I'M READY TO END THE SUSPENSE!
I'LL TELL YOU WHO WROTE THE LETTER!
IT DOESN'T MATTER, ARCHIE...
WE ALREADY KNOW...
AND WE THINK IT STINKS!
WITH A CAPITAL "S"!
AW, C'MON! IT'S NO BIG DEAL!
EASY FOR YOU TO SAY!
BUT I'M OFFICIALLY ENDING OUR FRIENDSHIP!
IT ENDED MINUTES AGO, TRAITOR!
GOOD-BYE!
?
GOOD-BYE!

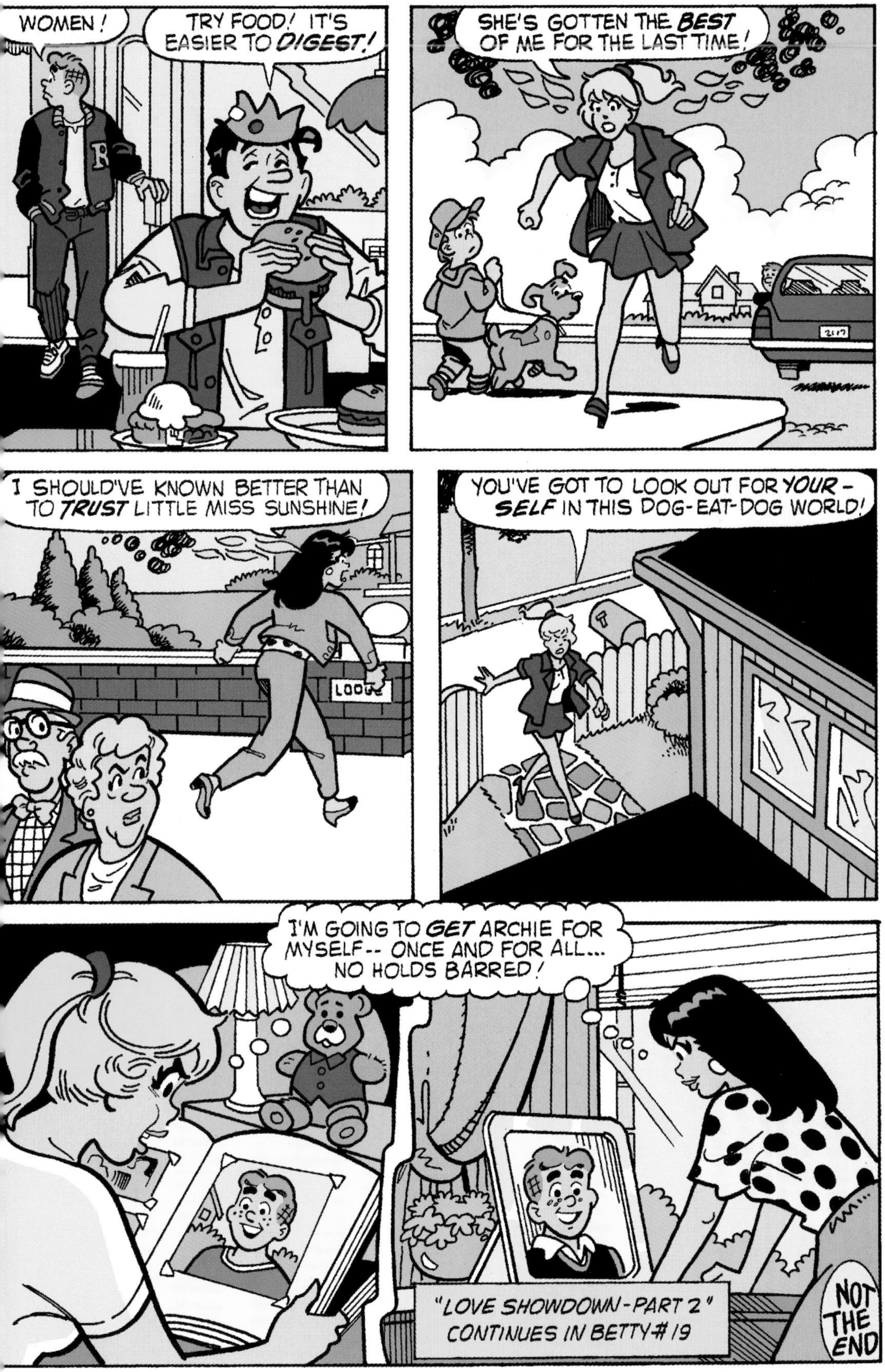
WOMEN!
TRY FOOD! IT'S EASIER TO DIGEST!
SHE'S GOTTEN THE BEST OF ME FOR THE LAST TIME!
I SHOULD'VE KNOWN BETTER THAN TO TRUST LITTLE MISS SUNSHINE!
LODGE
YOU'VE GOT TO LOOK OUT FOR YOURSELF IN THIS DOG-EAT-DOG WORLD!
I'M GOING TO GET ARCHIE FOR MYSELF-- ONCE AND FOR ALL... NO HOLDS BARRED!
"LOVE SHOWDOWN-PART 2" CONTINUES IN BETTY #19
NOT THE END

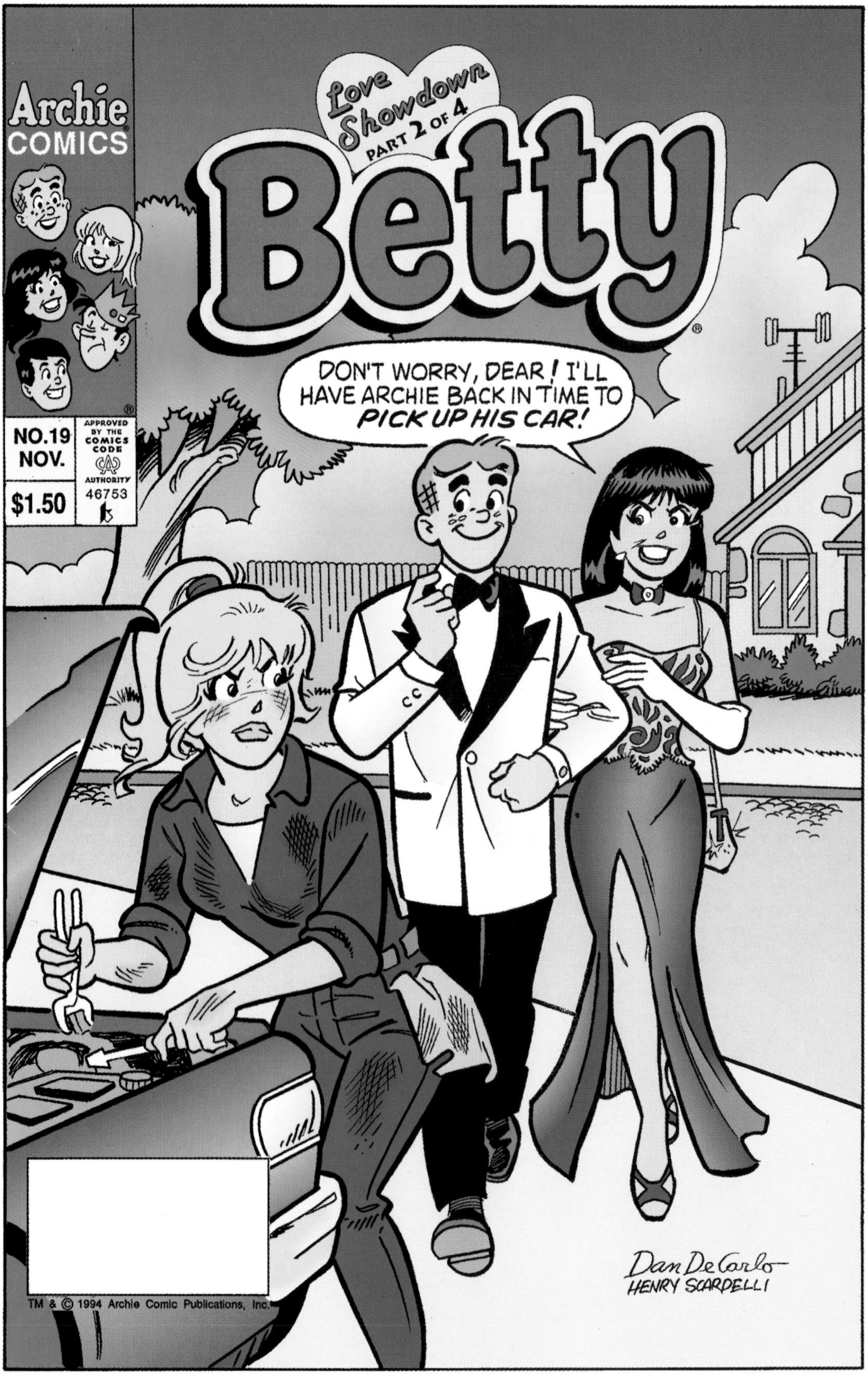

Archie COMICS
Love Showdown PART 2 OF 4
Betty
DON'T WORRY, DEAR! I'LL HAVE ARCHIE BACK IN TIME TO PICK UP HIS CAR!
NO.19 NOV.
$1.50
APPROVED BY THE COMICS CODE AUTHORITY
46753
Dan DeCarlo
HENRY SCARPELLI
TM & © 1994 Archie Comic Publications, Inc.

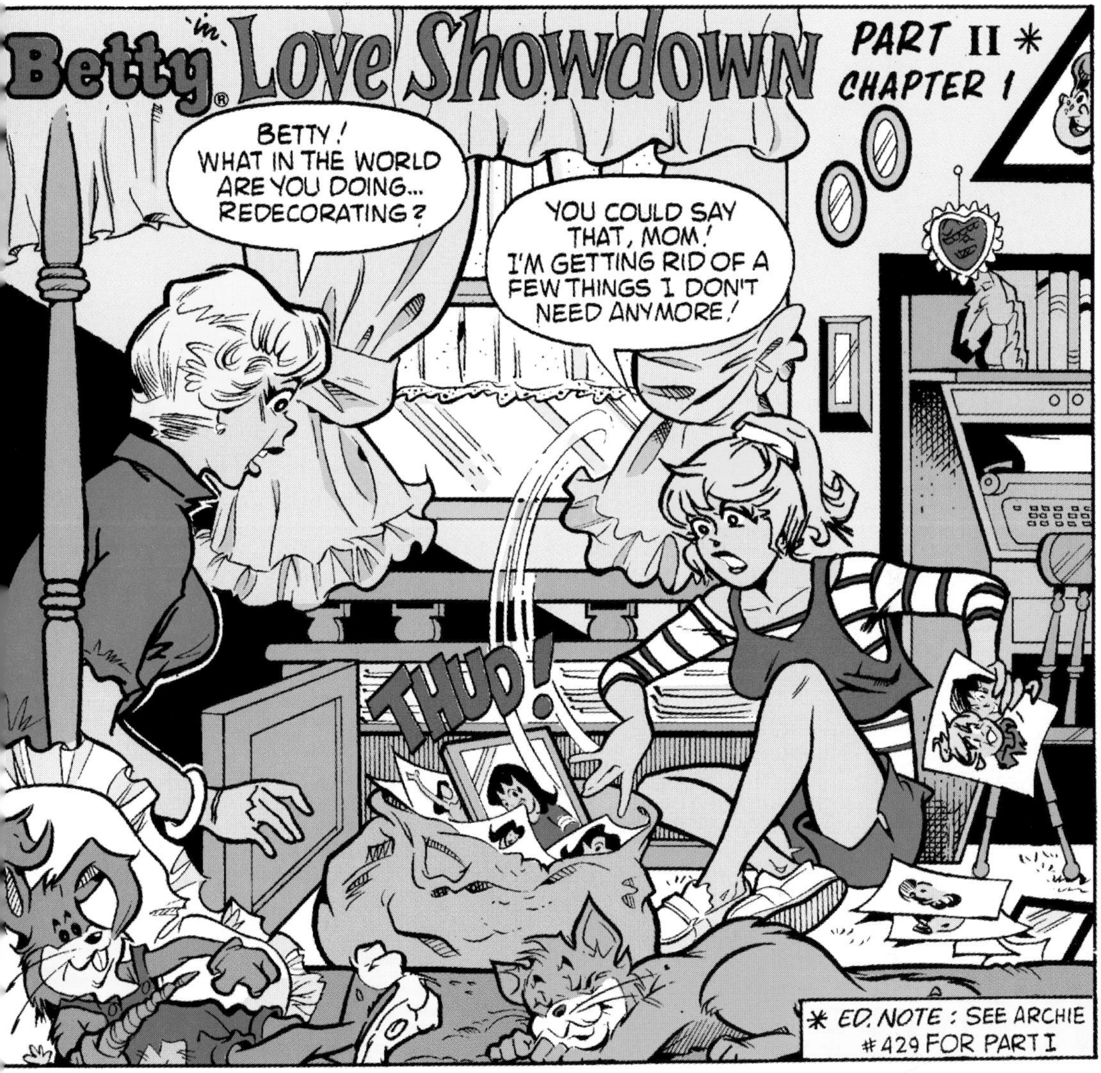

Betty -in- Love Showdown
PART II *
CHAPTER 1
BETTY! WHAT IN THE WORLD ARE YOU DOING... REDECORATING?
YOU COULD SAY THAT, MOM! I'M GETTING RID OF A FEW THINGS I DON'T NEED ANYMORE!
THUD!
* ED. NOTE: SEE ARCHIE #429 FOR PART I

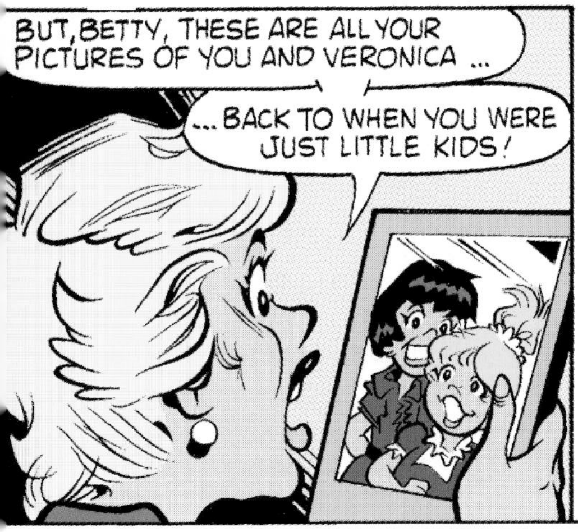

BUT, BETTY, THESE ARE ALL YOUR PICTURES OF YOU AND VERONICA ...
... BACK TO WHEN YOU WERE JUST LITTLE KIDS!

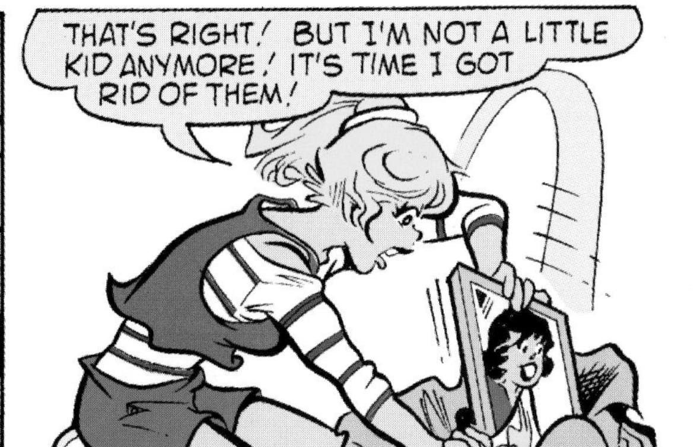

THAT'S RIGHT! BUT I'M NOT A LITTLE KID ANYMORE! IT'S TIME I GOT RID OF THEM!

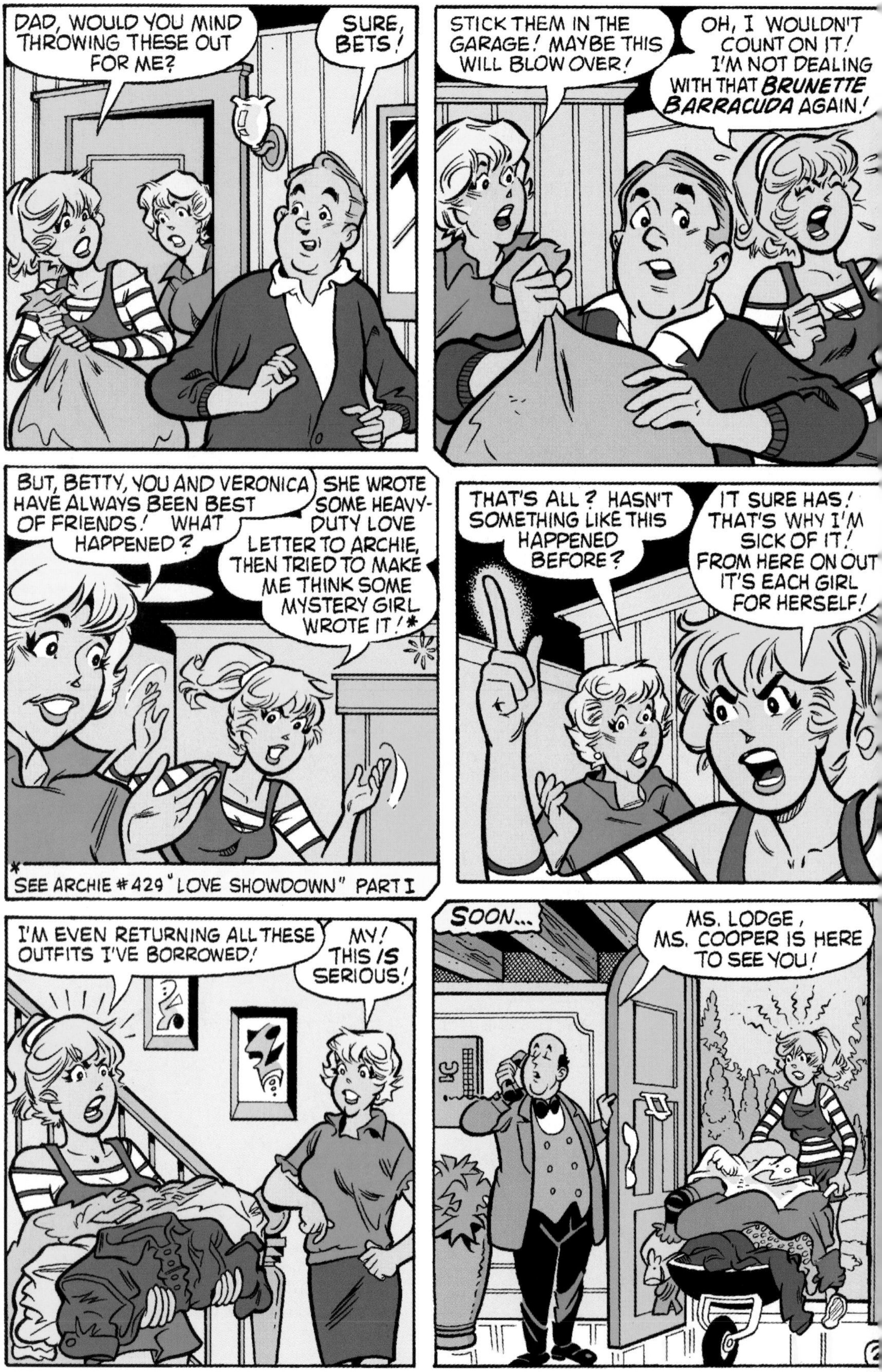
DAD, WOULD YOU MIND THROWING THESE OUT FOR ME?
SURE, BETS!
STICK THEM IN THE GARAGE! MAYBE THIS WILL BLOW OVER!
OH, I WOULDN'T COUNT ON IT! I'M NOT DEALING WITH THAT BRUNETTE BARRACUDA AGAIN!
BUT, BETTY, YOU AND VERONICA HAVE ALWAYS BEEN BEST OF FRIENDS! WHAT HAPPENED?
SHE WROTE SOME HEAVY-DUTY LOVE LETTER TO ARCHIE, THEN TRIED TO MAKE ME THINK SOME MYSTERY GIRL WROTE IT!*
*SEE ARCHIE #429 "LOVE SHOWDOWN" PART I
THAT'S ALL? HASN'T SOMETHING LIKE THIS HAPPENED BEFORE?
IT SURE HAS! THAT'S WHY I'M SICK OF IT! FROM HERE ON OUT IT'S EACH GIRL FOR HERSELF!
I'M EVEN RETURNING ALL THESE OUTFITS I'VE BORROWED!
MY! THIS IS SERIOUS!
SOON...
MS. LODGE, MS. COOPER IS HERE TO SEE YOU!

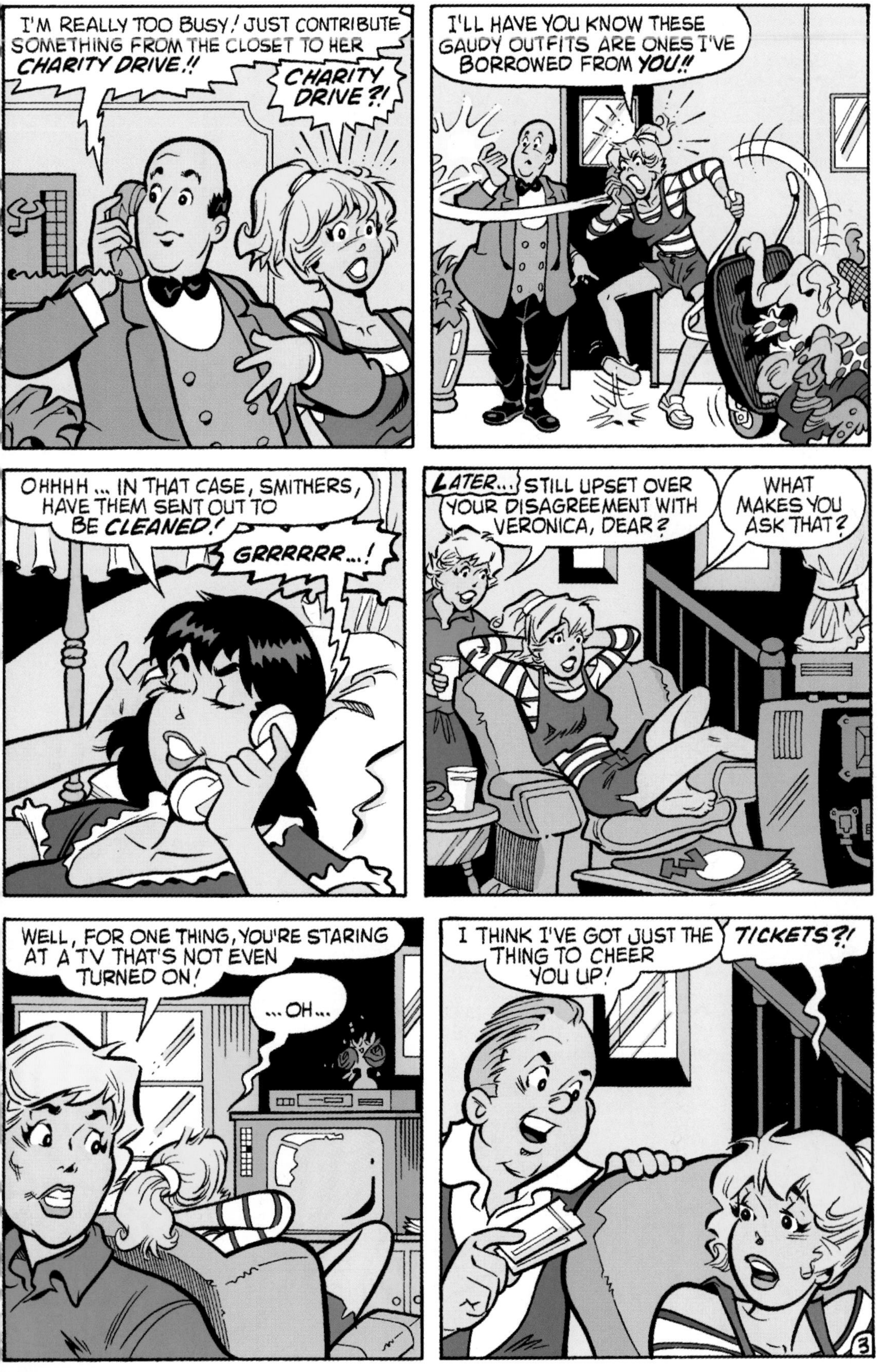
I'M REALLY TOO BUSY! JUST CONTRIBUTE SOMETHING FROM THE CLOSET TO HER CHARITY DRIVE!!
CHARITY DRIVE?!
I'LL HAVE YOU KNOW THESE GAUDY OUTFITS ARE ONES I'VE BORROWED FROM YOU!!
OHHHH ... IN THAT CASE, SMITHERS, HAVE THEM SENT OUT TO BE CLEANED!
GRRRRRR...!
LATER...
STILL UPSET OVER YOUR DISAGREEMENT WITH VERONICA, DEAR?
WHAT MAKES YOU ASK THAT?
WELL, FOR ONE THING, YOU'RE STARING AT A TV THAT'S NOT EVEN TURNED ON!
...OH...
I THINK I'VE GOT JUST THE THING TO CHEER YOU UP!
TICKETS?!
3

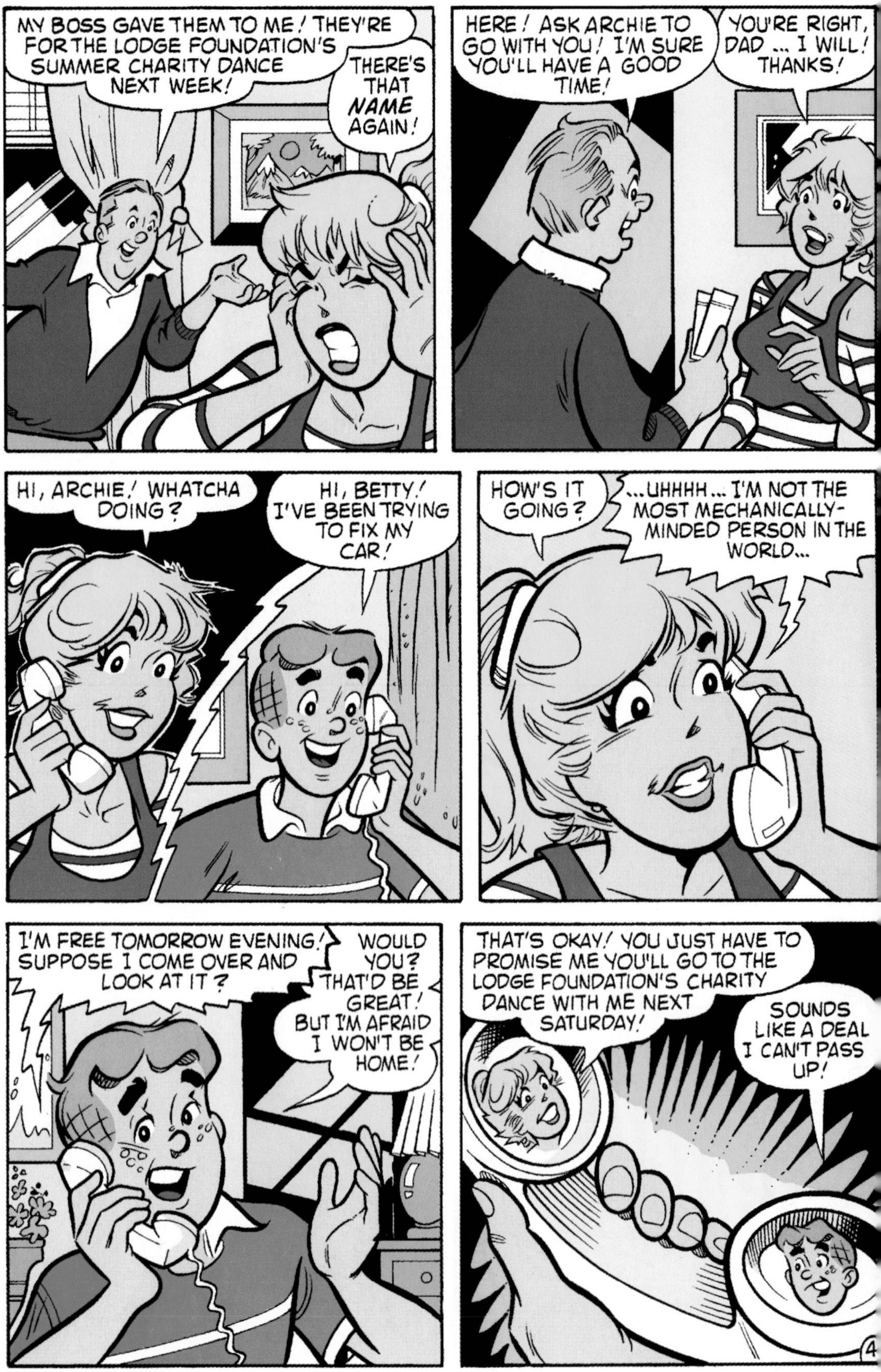
MY BOSS GAVE THEM TO ME! THEY'RE FOR THE LODGE FOUNDATION'S SUMMER CHARITY DANCE NEXT WEEK!
THERE'S THAT *NAME* AGAIN!
HERE! ASK ARCHIE TO GO WITH YOU! I'M SURE YOU'LL HAVE A GOOD TIME!
YOU'RE RIGHT, DAD ... I WILL! THANKS!
HI, ARCHIE! WHATCHA DOING?
HI, BETTY! I'VE BEEN TRYING TO FIX MY CAR!
HOW'S IT GOING?
...UHHHH ... I'M NOT THE MOST MECHANICALLY-MINDED PERSON IN THE WORLD...
I'M FREE TOMORROW EVENING! SUPPOSE I COME OVER AND LOOK AT IT?
WOULD YOU? THAT'D BE GREAT! BUT I'M AFRAID I WON'T BE HOME!
THAT'S OKAY! YOU JUST HAVE TO PROMISE ME YOU'LL GO TO THE LODGE FOUNDATION'S CHARITY DANCE WITH ME NEXT SATURDAY!
SOUNDS LIKE A DEAL I CAN'T PASS UP!
4

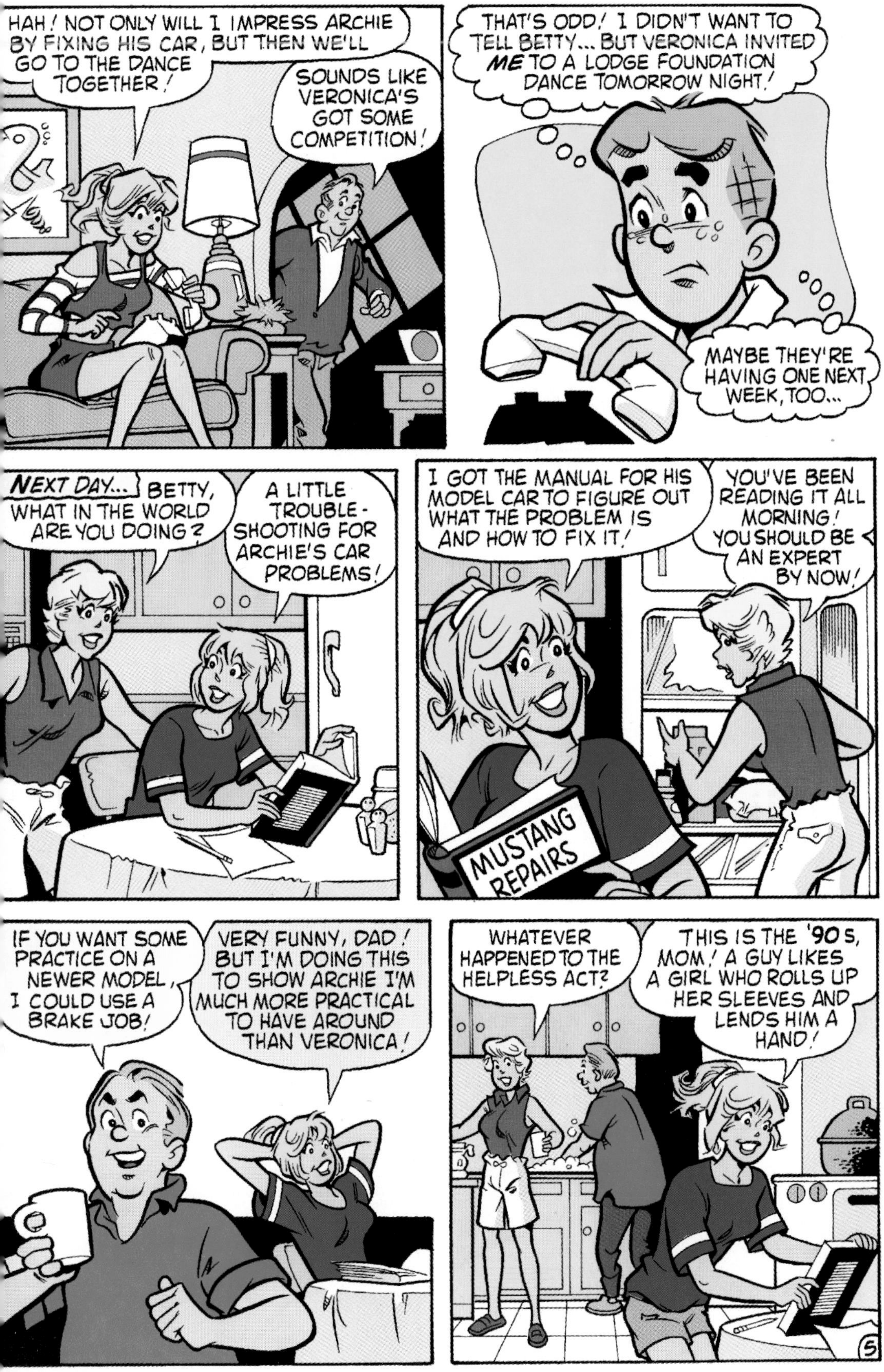

HAH! NOT ONLY WILL I IMPRESS ARCHIE BY FIXING HIS CAR, BUT THEN WE'LL GO TO THE DANCE TOGETHER!
SOUNDS LIKE VERONICA'S GOT SOME COMPETITION!
THAT'S ODD! I DIDN'T WANT TO TELL BETTY... BUT VERONICA INVITED ME TO A LODGE FOUNDATION DANCE TOMORROW NIGHT!
MAYBE THEY'RE HAVING ONE NEXT WEEK, TOO...
NEXT DAY...
BETTY, WHAT IN THE WORLD ARE YOU DOING?
A LITTLE TROUBLE-SHOOTING FOR ARCHIE'S CAR PROBLEMS!
I GOT THE MANUAL FOR HIS MODEL CAR TO FIGURE OUT WHAT THE PROBLEM IS AND HOW TO FIX IT!
YOU'VE BEEN READING IT ALL MORNING! YOU SHOULD BE AN EXPERT BY NOW!
MUSTANG REPAIRS
IF YOU WANT SOME PRACTICE ON A NEWER MODEL, I COULD USE A BRAKE JOB!
VERY FUNNY, DAD! BUT I'M DOING THIS TO SHOW ARCHIE I'M MUCH MORE PRACTICAL TO HAVE AROUND THAN VERONICA!
WHATEVER HAPPENED TO THE HELPLESS ACT?
THIS IS THE '90s, MOM! A GUY LIKES A GIRL WHO ROLLS UP HER SLEEVES AND LENDS HIM A HAND!
5

SEE YOU TWO LATER! I'VE GOT A JOB TO DO!

DO YOU THINK THE HOSPITAL GAVE US MR. GOODWRENCH'S BABY BY MISTAKE?

HI, ARCH! HOW'RE YOU DOING?

NOT TOO GOOD! THIS THING STILL HAS ME STUMPED...

WELL, I'VE BEEN DOING A LITTLE STUDYING AND I THINK I KNOW WHERE YOUR PROBLEM IS!

YOU'VE GOT TO BE KIDDING!

SOON... AH-HAH! JUST AS I THOUGHT!

WHAT IS IT?

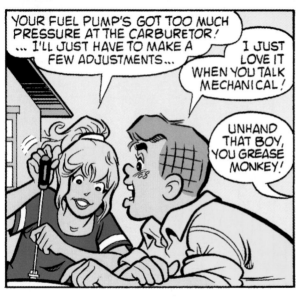

YOUR FUEL PUMP'S GOT TOO MUCH PRESSURE AT THE CARBURETOR! ...I'LL JUST HAVE TO MAKE A FEW ADJUSTMENTS...

I JUST LOVE IT WHEN YOU TALK MECHANICAL!

UNHAND THAT BOY, YOU GREASE MONKEY!

I'VE GOT DIBS ON HIM TONIGHT!

VERONICA!?!

CONTINUED...

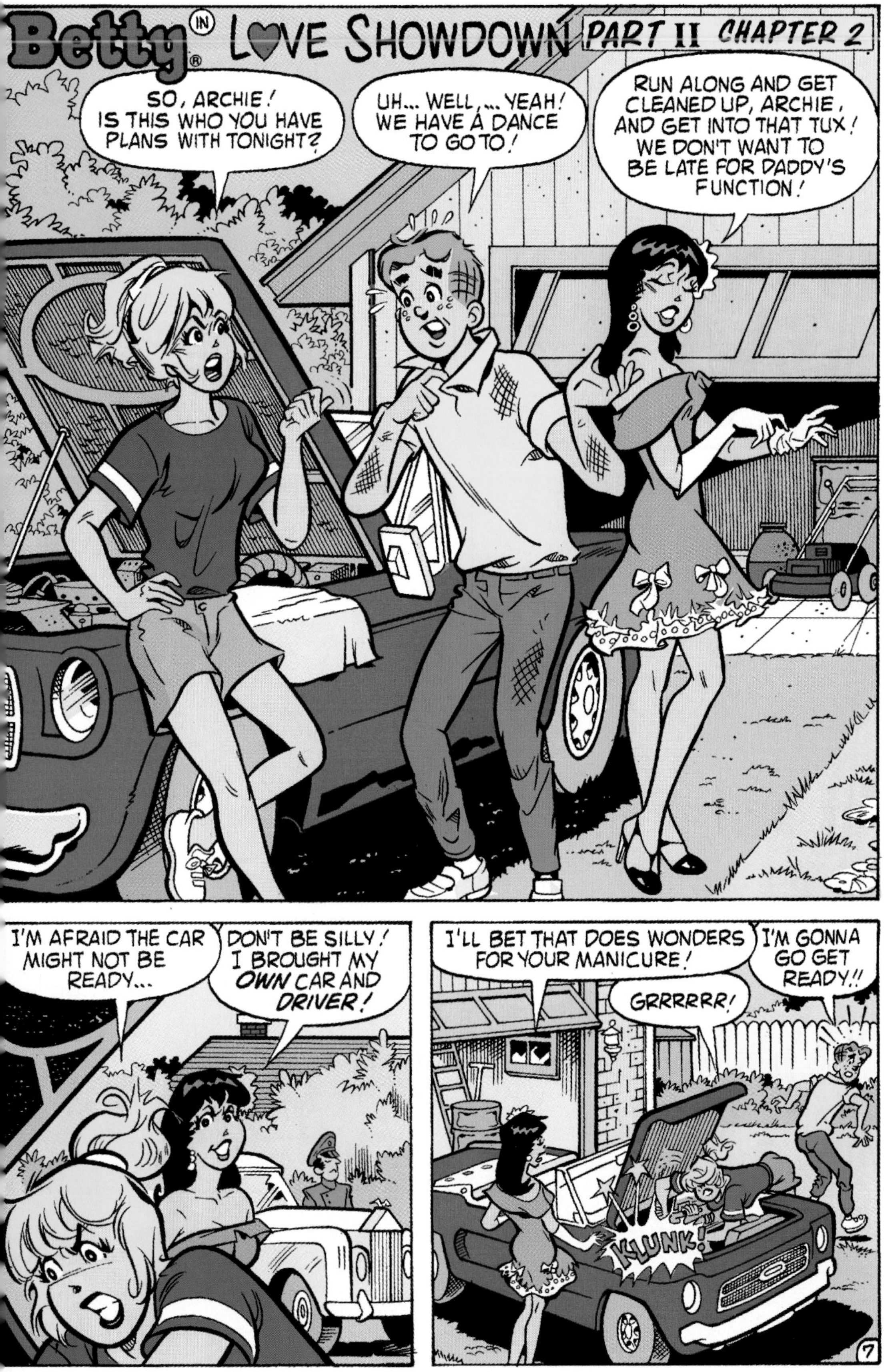
Betty IN LOVE SHOWDOWN PART II CHAPTER 2
SO, ARCHIE! IS THIS WHO YOU HAVE PLANS WITH TONIGHT?
UH... WELL, ... YEAH! WE HAVE A DANCE TO GO TO!
RUN ALONG AND GET CLEANED UP, ARCHIE, AND GET INTO THAT TUX! WE DON'T WANT TO BE LATE FOR DADDY'S FUNCTION!
I'M AFRAID THE CAR MIGHT NOT BE READY...
DON'T BE SILLY! I BROUGHT MY OWN CAR AND DRIVER!
I'LL BET THAT DOES WONDERS FOR YOUR MANICURE!
I'M GONNA GO GET READY!!
GRRRRRR!
KLUNK!
7

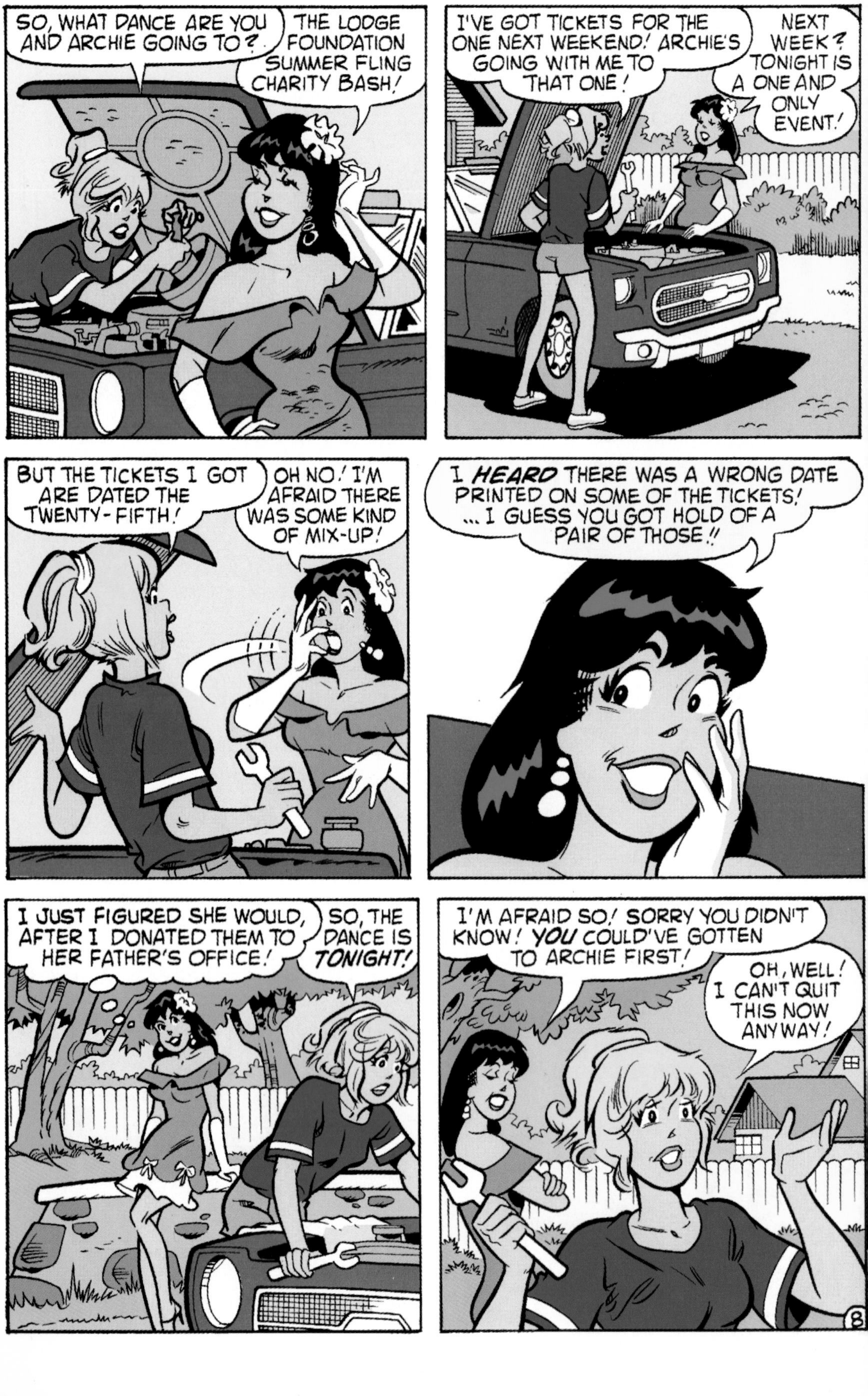

SO, WHAT DANCE ARE YOU AND ARCHIE GOING TO?
THE LODGE FOUNDATION SUMMER FLING CHARITY BASH!
I'VE GOT TICKETS FOR THE ONE NEXT WEEKEND! ARCHIE'S GOING WITH ME TO THAT ONE!
NEXT WEEK? TONIGHT IS A ONE AND ONLY EVENT!
BUT THE TICKETS I GOT ARE DATED THE TWENTY-FIFTH!
OH NO! I'M AFRAID THERE WAS SOME KIND OF MIX-UP!
I HEARD THERE WAS A WRONG DATE PRINTED ON SOME OF THE TICKETS! ... I GUESS YOU GOT HOLD OF A PAIR OF THOSE!!
I JUST FIGURED SHE WOULD, AFTER I DONATED THEM TO HER FATHER'S OFFICE!
SO, THE DANCE IS TONIGHT!
I'M AFRAID SO! SORRY YOU DIDN'T KNOW! YOU COULD'VE GOTTEN TO ARCHIE FIRST!
OH, WELL! I CAN'T QUIT THIS NOW ANYWAY!
8

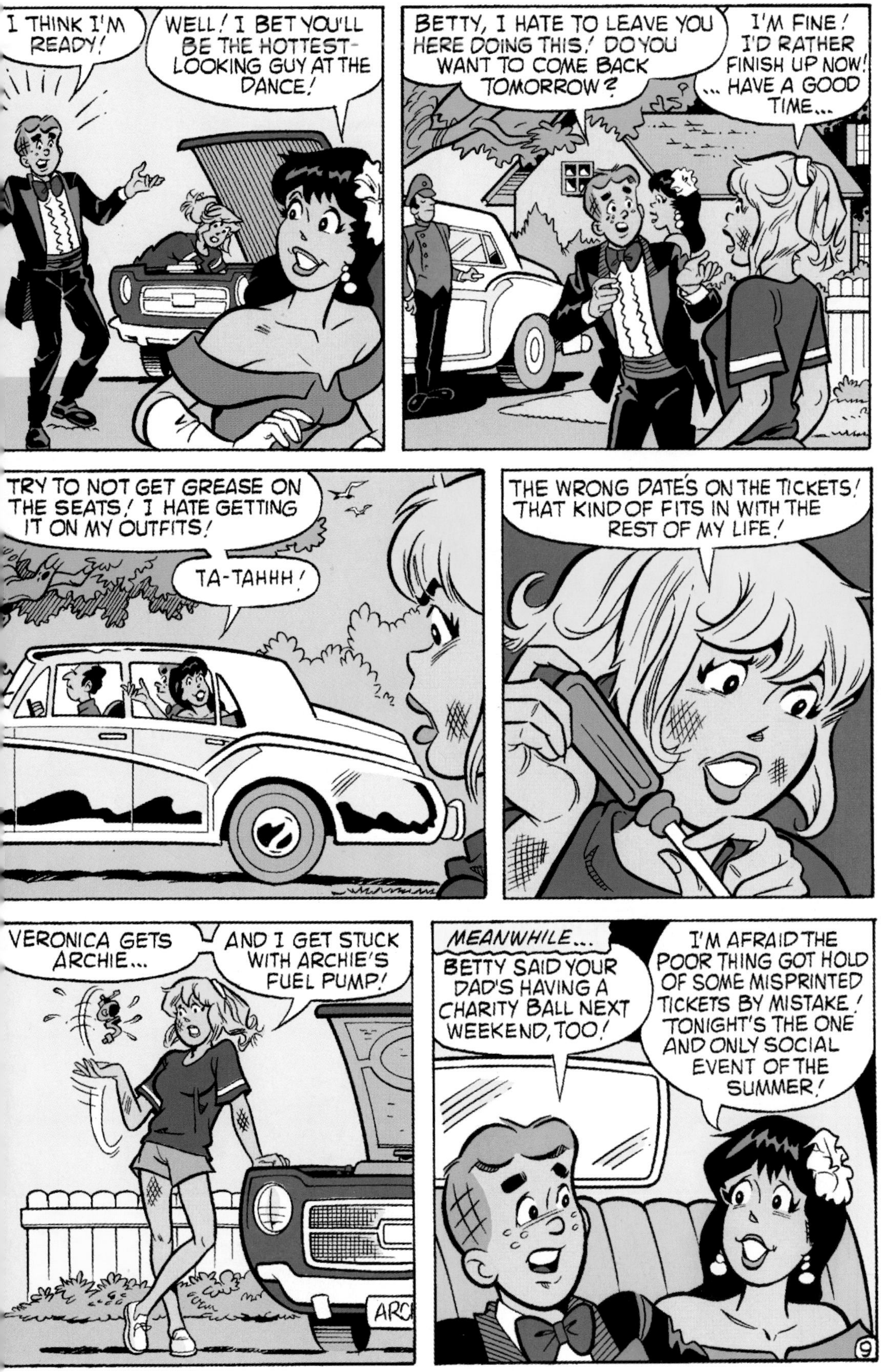

I THINK I'M READY!
WELL! I BET YOU'LL BE THE HOTTEST-LOOKING GUY AT THE DANCE!
BETTY, I HATE TO LEAVE YOU HERE DOING THIS! DO YOU WANT TO COME BACK TOMORROW?
I'M FINE! I'D RATHER FINISH UP NOW! ... HAVE A GOOD TIME...
TRY TO NOT GET GREASE ON THE SEATS! I HATE GETTING IT ON MY OUTFITS!
TA-TAHHH!
THE WRONG DATE'S ON THE TICKETS! THAT KIND OF FITS IN WITH THE REST OF MY LIFE!
VERONICA GETS ARCHIE...
AND I GET STUCK WITH ARCHIE'S FUEL PUMP!
ARC
MEANWHILE...
BETTY SAID YOUR DAD'S HAVING A CHARITY BALL NEXT WEEKEND, TOO!
I'M AFRAID THE POOR THING GOT HOLD OF SOME MISPRINTED TICKETS BY MISTAKE! TONIGHT'S THE ONE AND ONLY SOCIAL EVENT OF THE SUMMER!
9

SOON: THERE! IT'S RUNNING LIKE A TOP! BETTY COOPER TO THE RESCUE AGAIN!

PURRRRRRRRRRRRR

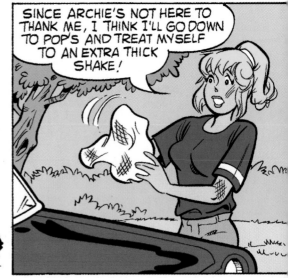

SINCE ARCHIE'S NOT HERE TO THANK ME, I THINK I'LL GO DOWN TO POP'S AND TREAT MYSELF TO AN EXTRA THICK SHAKE!

AND SO... SI-I-I-GH!

HI, BETTY! WHY SO GRIM?

POP'S SPECIAL

ARCHIE AND VERONICA ARE AT HER FATHER'S CHARITY DANCE TONIGHT ...AND I'M HERE!!

PERSONALLY, I CAN'T THINK OF A BETTER PLACE TO BE!

Fries

IT SEEMS I GOT TICKETS WITH THE WRONG DATE ON THEM!

HMMMM! LET ME SEE THOSE!

POP'S

YEAH! I WAS AT THE COPY CENTER WHEN VERONICA GOT THESE PRINTED UP!

WHAT?!

IC

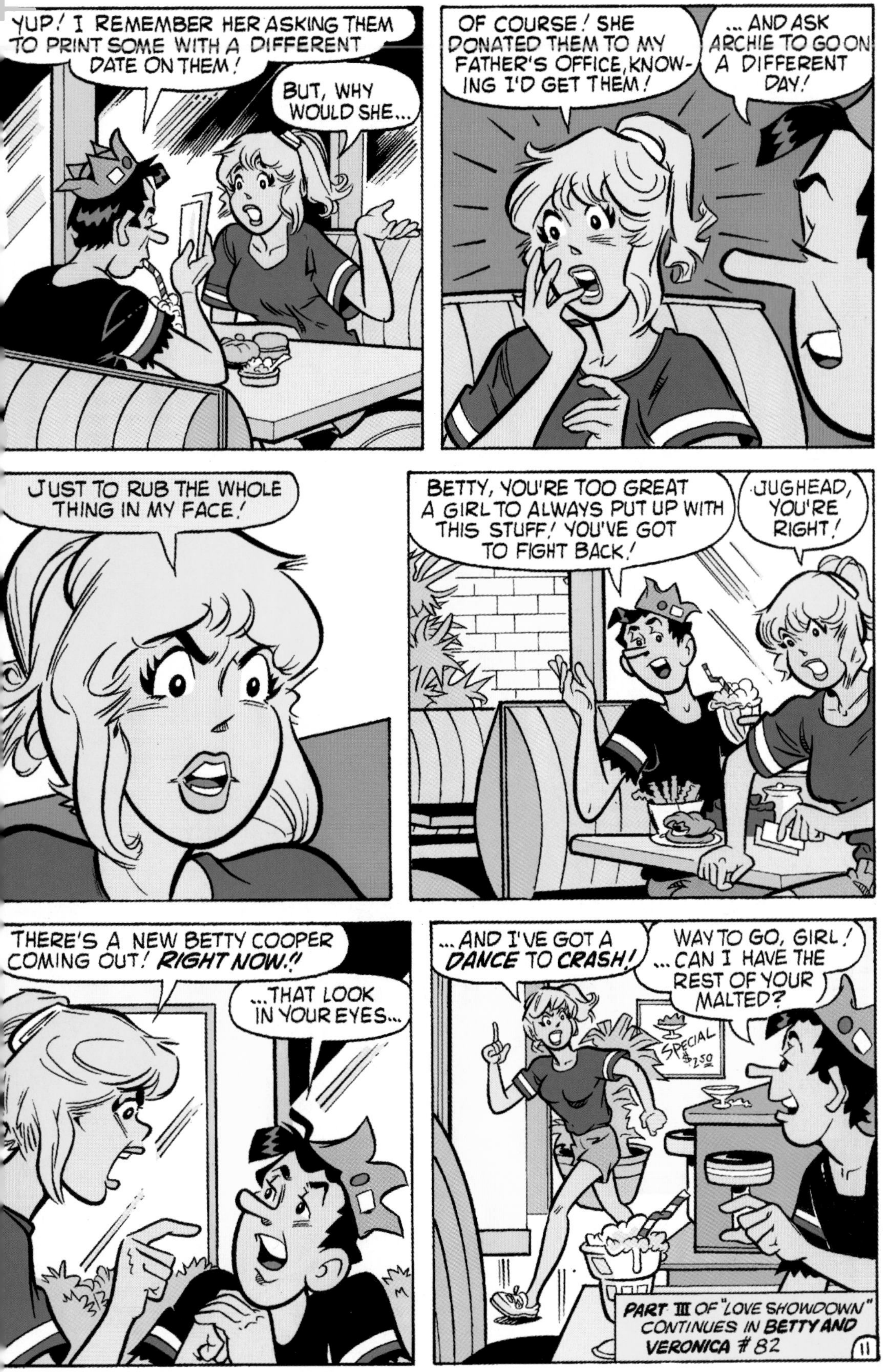
YUP! I REMEMBER HER ASKING THEM TO PRINT SOME WITH A DIFFERENT DATE ON THEM!
BUT, WHY WOULD SHE...
OF COURSE! SHE DONATED THEM TO MY FATHER'S OFFICE, KNOWING I'D GET THEM!
...AND ASK ARCHIE TO GO ON A DIFFERENT DAY!
JUST TO RUB THE WHOLE THING IN MY FACE!
BETTY, YOU'RE TOO GREAT A GIRL TO ALWAYS PUT UP WITH THIS STUFF! YOU'VE GOT TO FIGHT BACK!
JUGHEAD, YOU'RE RIGHT!
THERE'S A NEW BETTY COOPER COMING OUT! RIGHT NOW!!
...THAT LOOK IN YOUR EYES...
...AND I'VE GOT A DANCE TO CRASH!
WAY TO GO, GIRL! ...CAN I HAVE THE REST OF YOUR MALTED?
SPECIAL $2.50
PART III OF "LOVE SHOWDOWN" CONTINUES IN BETTY AND VERONICA #82
11

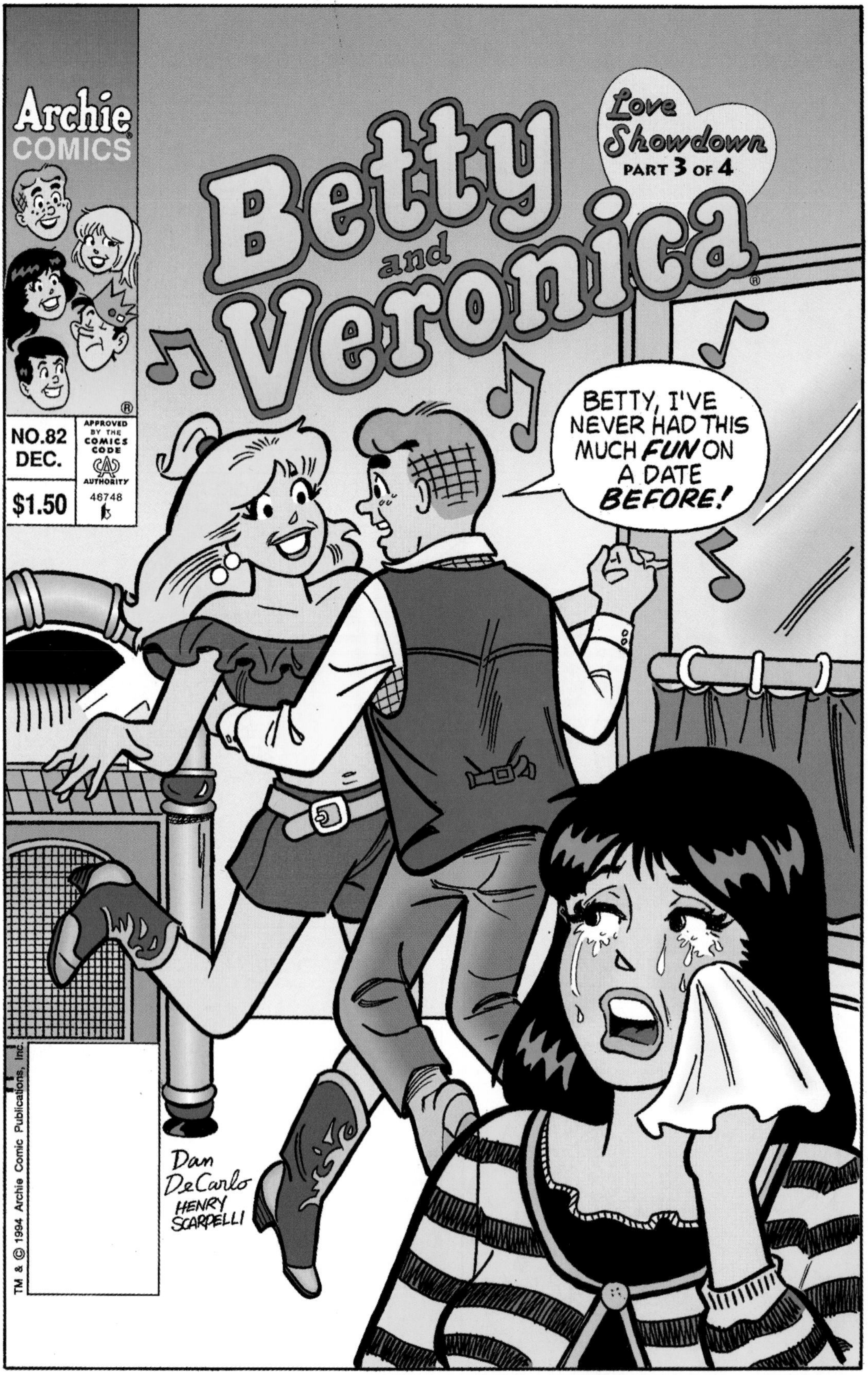
Archie COMICS
Betty and Veronica
Love Showdown PART 3 OF 4
NO.82 DEC.
$1.50
APPROVED BY THE COMICS CODE AUTHORITY
46748
BETTY, I'VE NEVER HAD THIS MUCH FUN ON A DATE BEFORE!
Dan DeCarlo HENRY SCARPELLI
TM & © 1994 Archie Comic Publications, Inc.

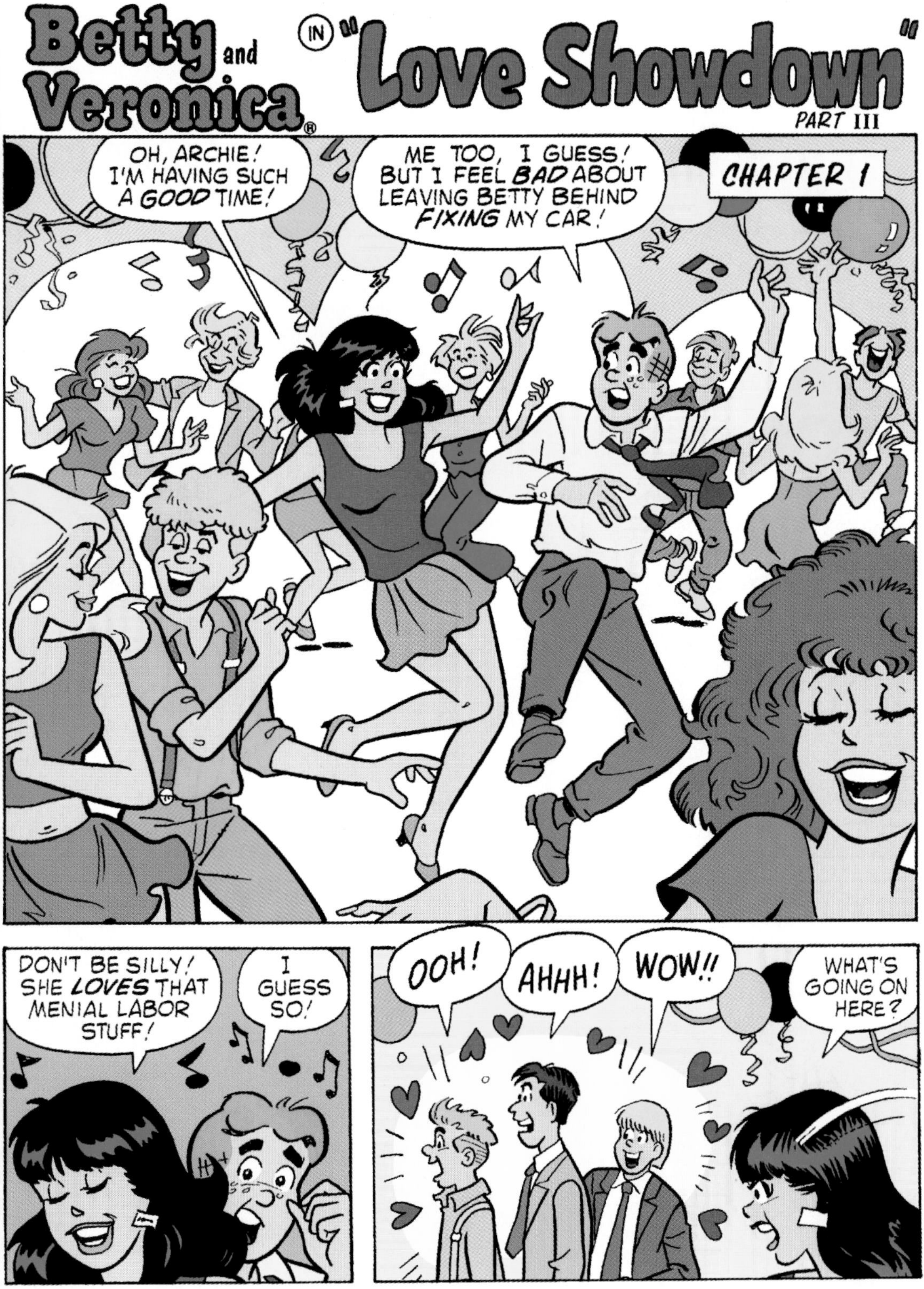
Betty and Veronica
IN "Love Showdown"
PART III
CHAPTER 1
OH, ARCHIE! I'M HAVING SUCH A GOOD TIME!
ME TOO, I GUESS! BUT I FEEL BAD ABOUT LEAVING BETTY BEHIND FIXING MY CAR!
DON'T BE SILLY! SHE LOVES THAT MENIAL LABOR STUFF!
I GUESS SO!
OOH!
AHHH!
WOW!!
WHAT'S GOING ON HERE?

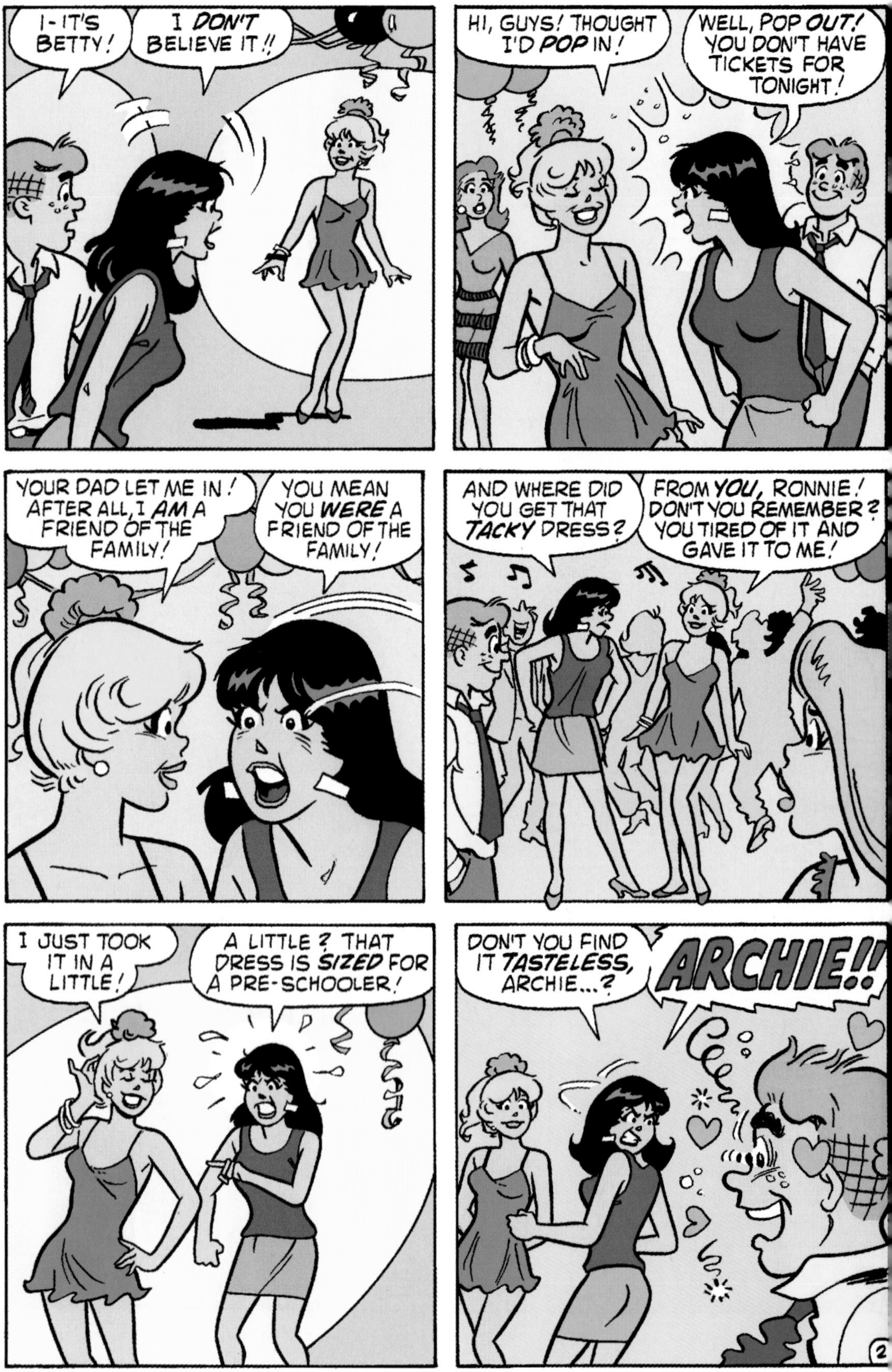

I- IT'S BETTY!
I DON'T BELIEVE IT!!
HI, GUYS! THOUGHT I'D POP IN!
WELL, POP OUT! YOU DON'T HAVE TICKETS FOR TONIGHT!
YOUR DAD LET ME IN! AFTER ALL, I AM A FRIEND OF THE FAMILY!
YOU MEAN YOU WERE A FRIEND OF THE FAMILY!
AND WHERE DID YOU GET THAT TACKY DRESS?
FROM YOU, RONNIE! DON'T YOU REMEMBER? YOU TIRED OF IT AND GAVE IT TO ME!
I JUST TOOK IT IN A LITTLE!
A LITTLE? THAT DRESS IS SIZED FOR A PRE-SCHOOLER!
DON'T YOU FIND IT TASTELESS, ARCHIE...?
ARCHIE!!

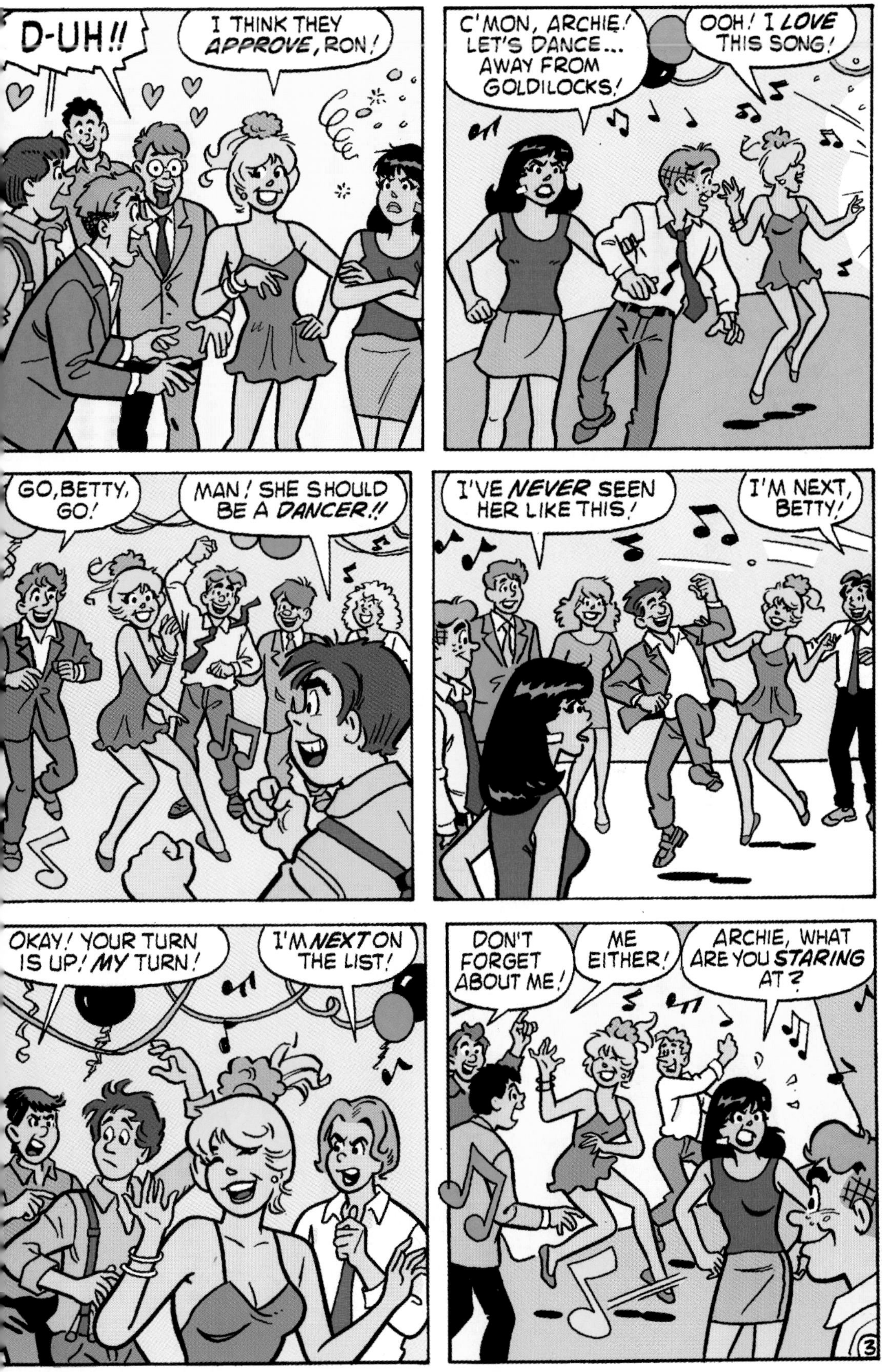
D-UH!!
I THINK THEY APPROVE, RON!
C'MON, ARCHIE! LET'S DANCE... AWAY FROM GOLDILOCKS!
OOH! I LOVE THIS SONG!
GO, BETTY, GO!
MAN! SHE SHOULD BE A DANCER!!
I'VE NEVER SEEN HER LIKE THIS!
I'M NEXT, BETTY!
OKAY! YOUR TURN IS UP! MY TURN!
I'M NEXT ON THE LIST!
DON'T FORGET ABOUT ME!
ME EITHER!
ARCHIE, WHAT ARE YOU STARING AT?
3

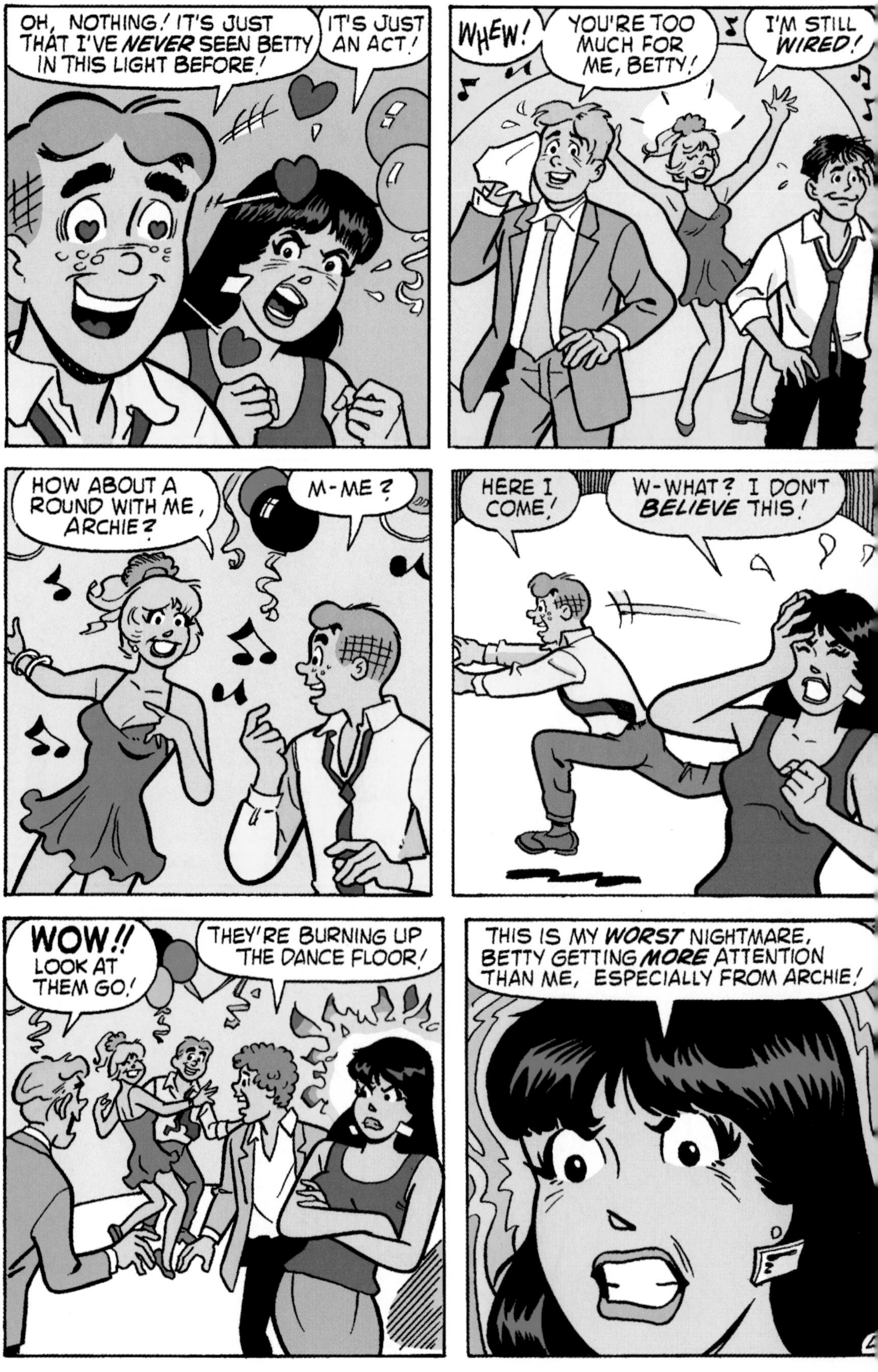

OH, NOTHING! IT'S JUST THAT I'VE NEVER SEEN BETTY IN THIS LIGHT BEFORE!
IT'S JUST AN ACT!
WHEW!
YOU'RE TOO MUCH FOR ME, BETTY!
I'M STILL WIRED!
HOW ABOUT A ROUND WITH ME, ARCHIE?
M-ME?
HERE I COME!
W-WHAT? I DON'T BELIEVE THIS!
WOW!! LOOK AT THEM GO!
THEY'RE BURNING UP THE DANCE FLOOR!
THIS IS MY WORST NIGHTMARE, BETTY GETTING MORE ATTENTION THAN ME, ESPECIALLY FROM ARCHIE!

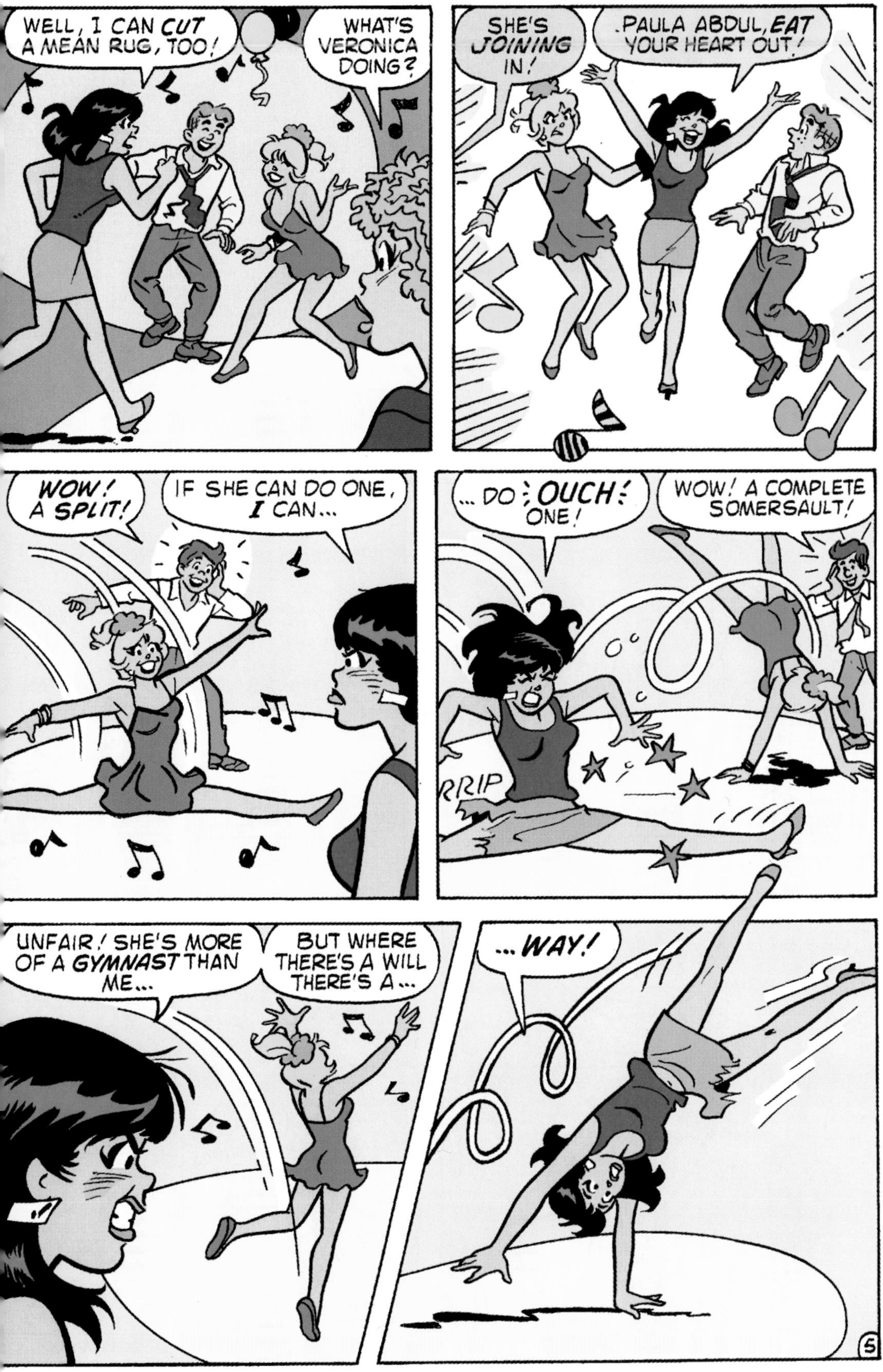
WELL, I CAN CUT A MEAN RUG, TOO!
WHAT'S VERONICA DOING?
SHE'S JOINING IN!
PAULA ABDUL, EAT YOUR HEART OUT!
WOW! A SPLIT!
IF SHE CAN DO ONE, I CAN...
... DO ; OUCH! ONE!
WOW! A COMPLETE SOMERSAULT!
RRIP
UNFAIR! SHE'S MORE OF A GYMNAST THAN ME...
BUT WHERE THERE'S A WILL THERE'S A...
... WAY!
5

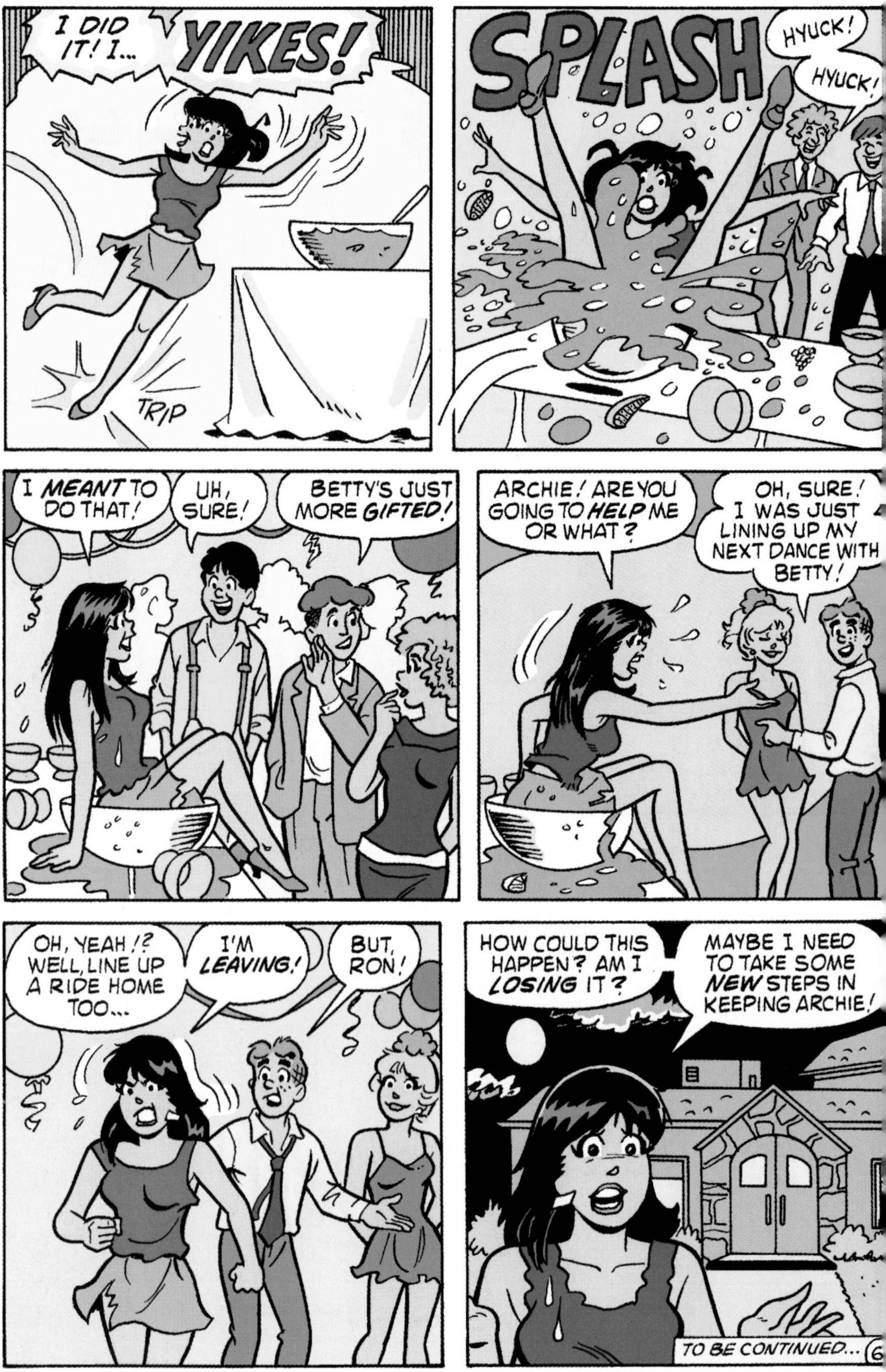
I DID IT! I...
YIKES!
TRIP
SPLASH
HYUCK!
HYUCK!
I MEANT TO DO THAT!
UH, SURE!
BETTY'S JUST MORE GIFTED!
ARCHIE! ARE YOU GOING TO HELP ME OR WHAT?
OH, SURE! I WAS JUST LINING UP MY NEXT DANCE WITH BETTY!
OH, YEAH!? WELL, LINE UP A RIDE HOME TOO...
I'M LEAVING!
BUT, RON!
HOW COULD THIS HAPPEN? AM I LOSING IT?
MAYBE I NEED TO TAKE SOME NEW STEPS IN KEEPING ARCHIE!
TO BE CONTINUED...
6

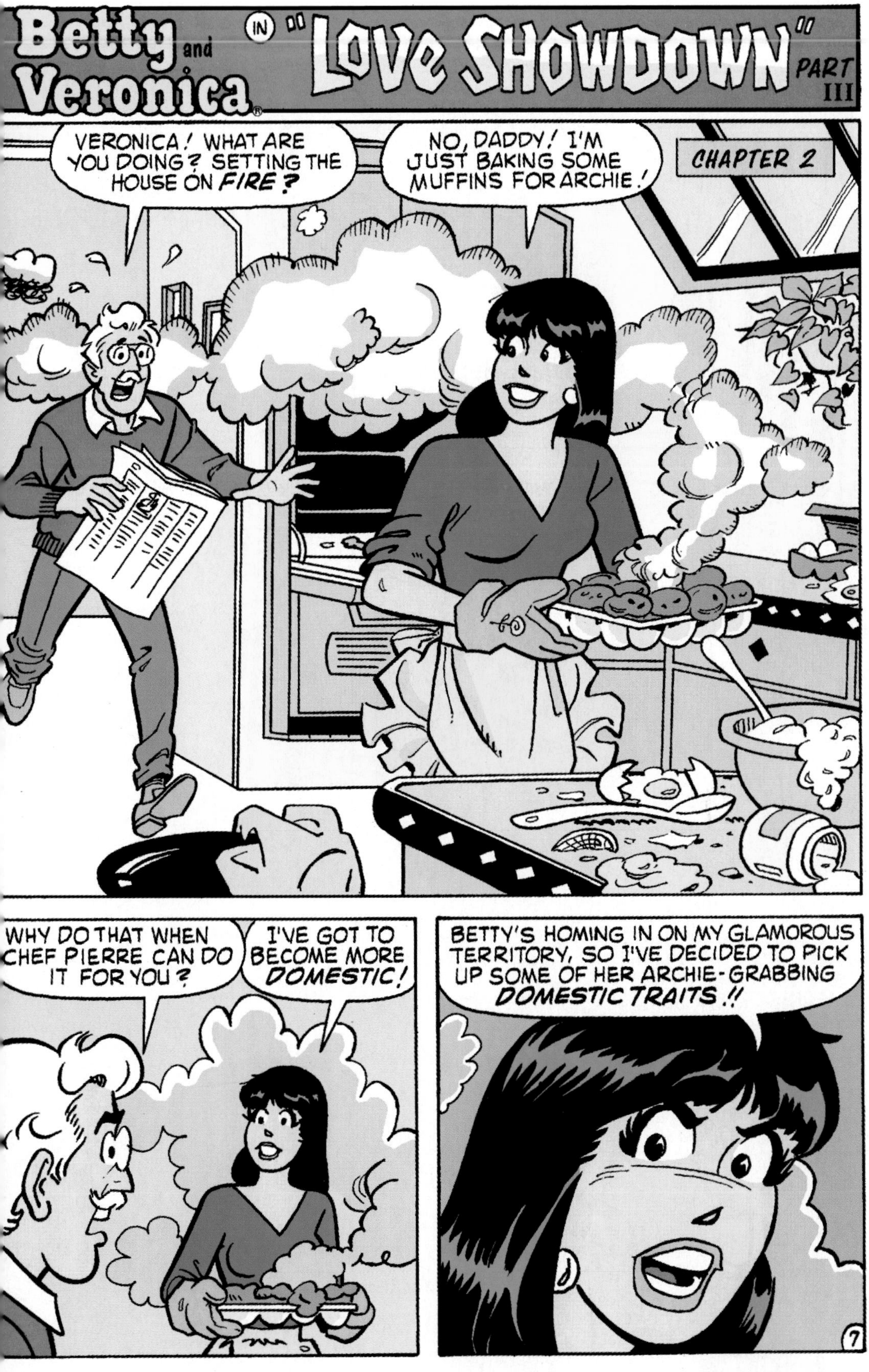
Betty and Veronica
IN "LOVE SHOWDOWN" PART III
VERONICA! WHAT ARE YOU DOING? SETTING THE HOUSE ON *FIRE?*
NO, DADDY! I'M JUST BAKING SOME MUFFINS FOR ARCHIE!
CHAPTER 2
WHY DO THAT WHEN CHEF PIERRE CAN DO IT FOR YOU?
I'VE GOT TO BECOME MORE *DOMESTIC!*
BETTY'S HOMING IN ON MY GLAMOROUS TERRITORY, SO I'VE DECIDED TO PICK UP SOME OF HER ARCHIE-GRABBING *DOMESTIC TRAITS!!*
7

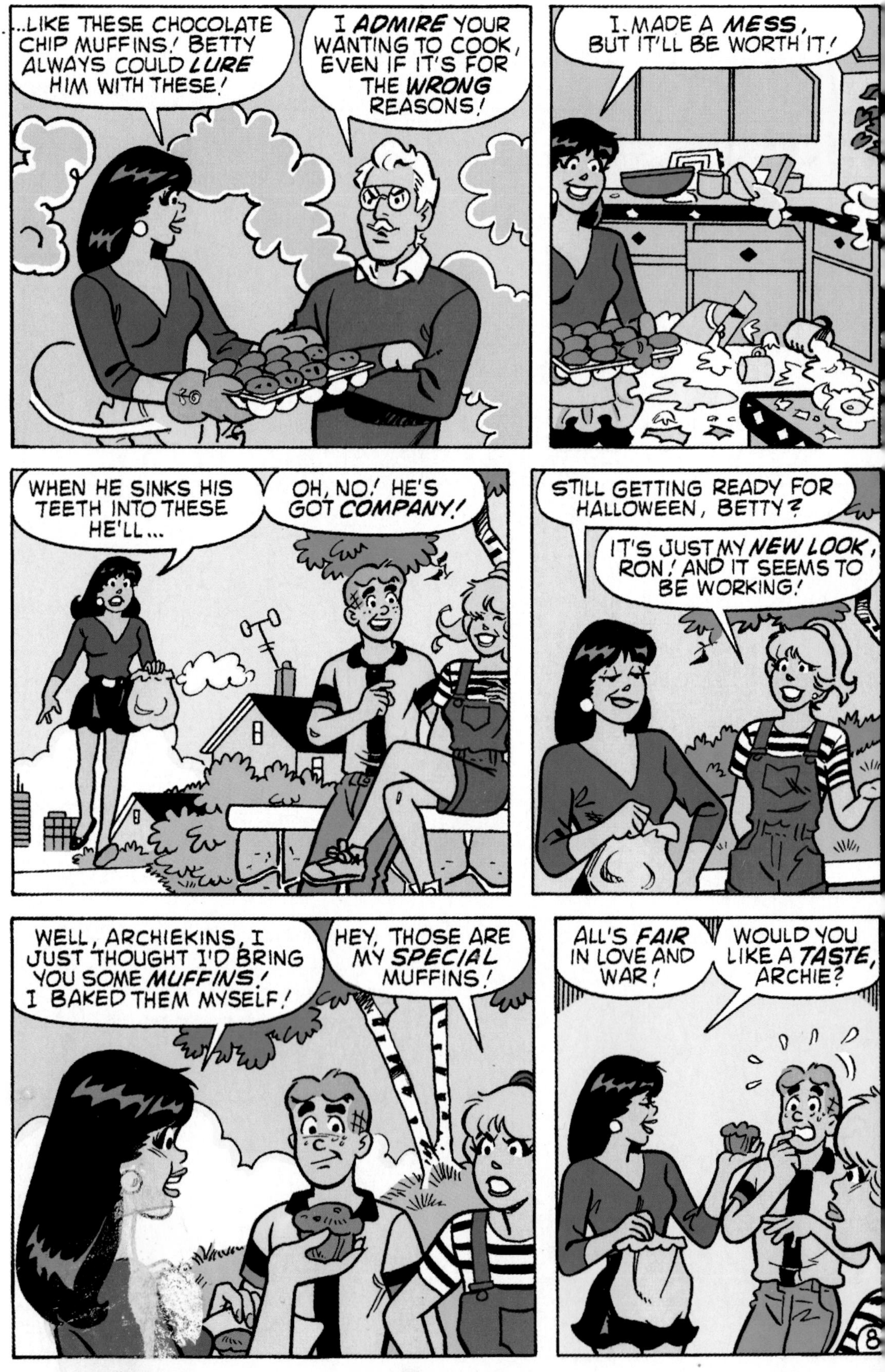
...LIKE THESE CHOCOLATE CHIP MUFFINS! BETTY ALWAYS COULD LURE HIM WITH THESE!
I ADMIRE YOUR WANTING TO COOK, EVEN IF IT'S FOR THE WRONG REASONS!
I MADE A MESS, BUT IT'LL BE WORTH IT!
WHEN HE SINKS HIS TEETH INTO THESE HE'LL...
OH, NO! HE'S GOT COMPANY!
STILL GETTING READY FOR HALLOWEEN, BETTY?
IT'S JUST MY NEW LOOK, RON! AND IT SEEMS TO BE WORKING!
WELL, ARCHIEKINS, I JUST THOUGHT I'D BRING YOU SOME MUFFINS! I BAKED THEM MYSELF!
HEY, THOSE ARE MY SPECIAL MUFFINS!
ALL'S FAIR IN LOVE AND WAR!
WOULD YOU LIKE A TASTE, ARCHIE?
8

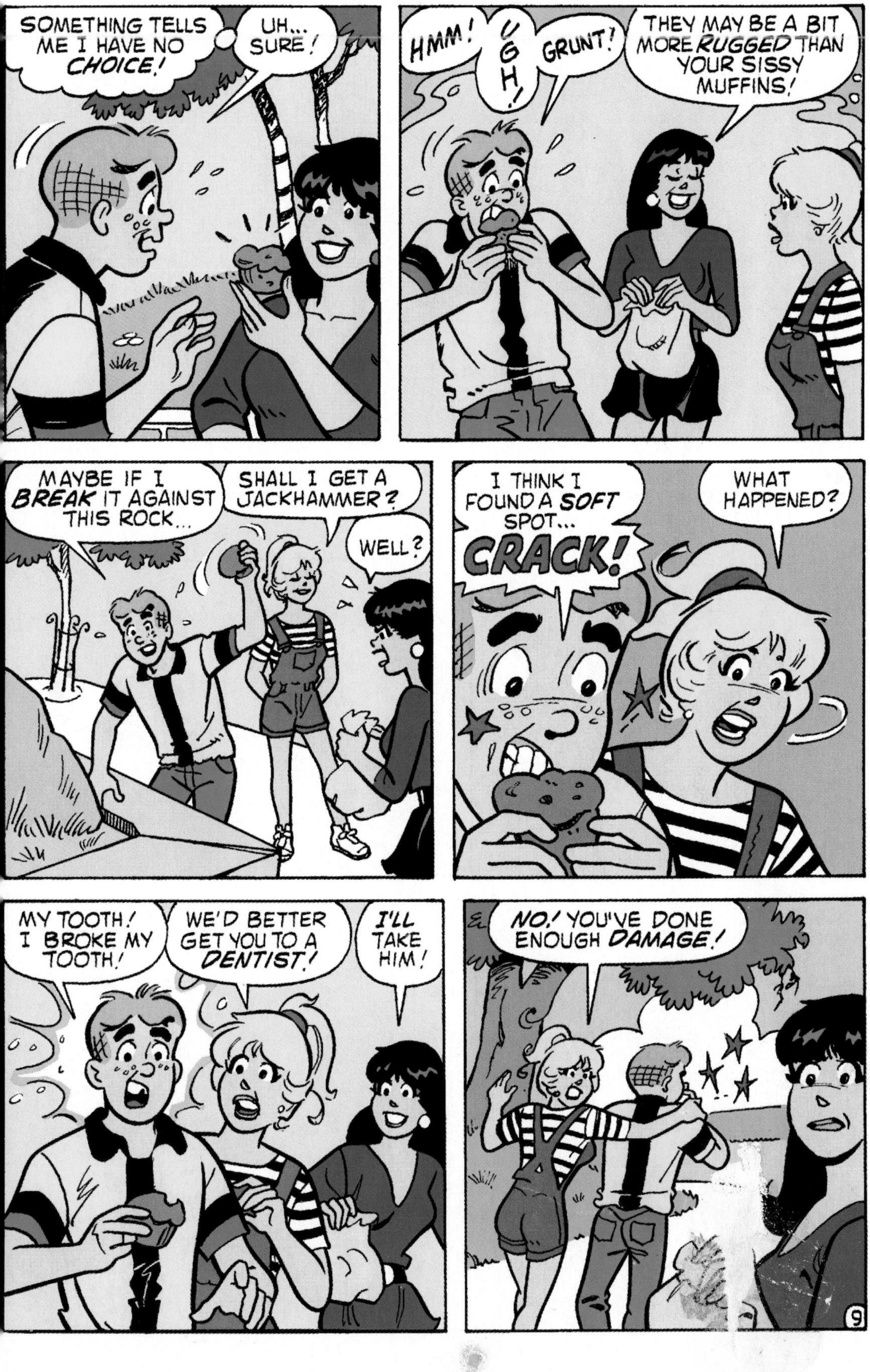
SOMETHING TELLS ME I HAVE NO CHOICE!
UH... SURE!
HMM!
UGH!
GRUNT!
THEY MAY BE A BIT MORE RUGGED THAN YOUR SISSY MUFFINS!
MAYBE IF I BREAK IT AGAINST THIS ROCK...
SHALL I GET A JACKHAMMER?
WELL?
I THINK I FOUND A SOFT SPOT...
CRACK!
WHAT HAPPENED?
MY TOOTH! I BROKE MY TOOTH!
WE'D BETTER GET YOU TO A DENTIST!
I'LL TAKE HIM!
NO! YOU'VE DONE ENOUGH DAMAGE!
9

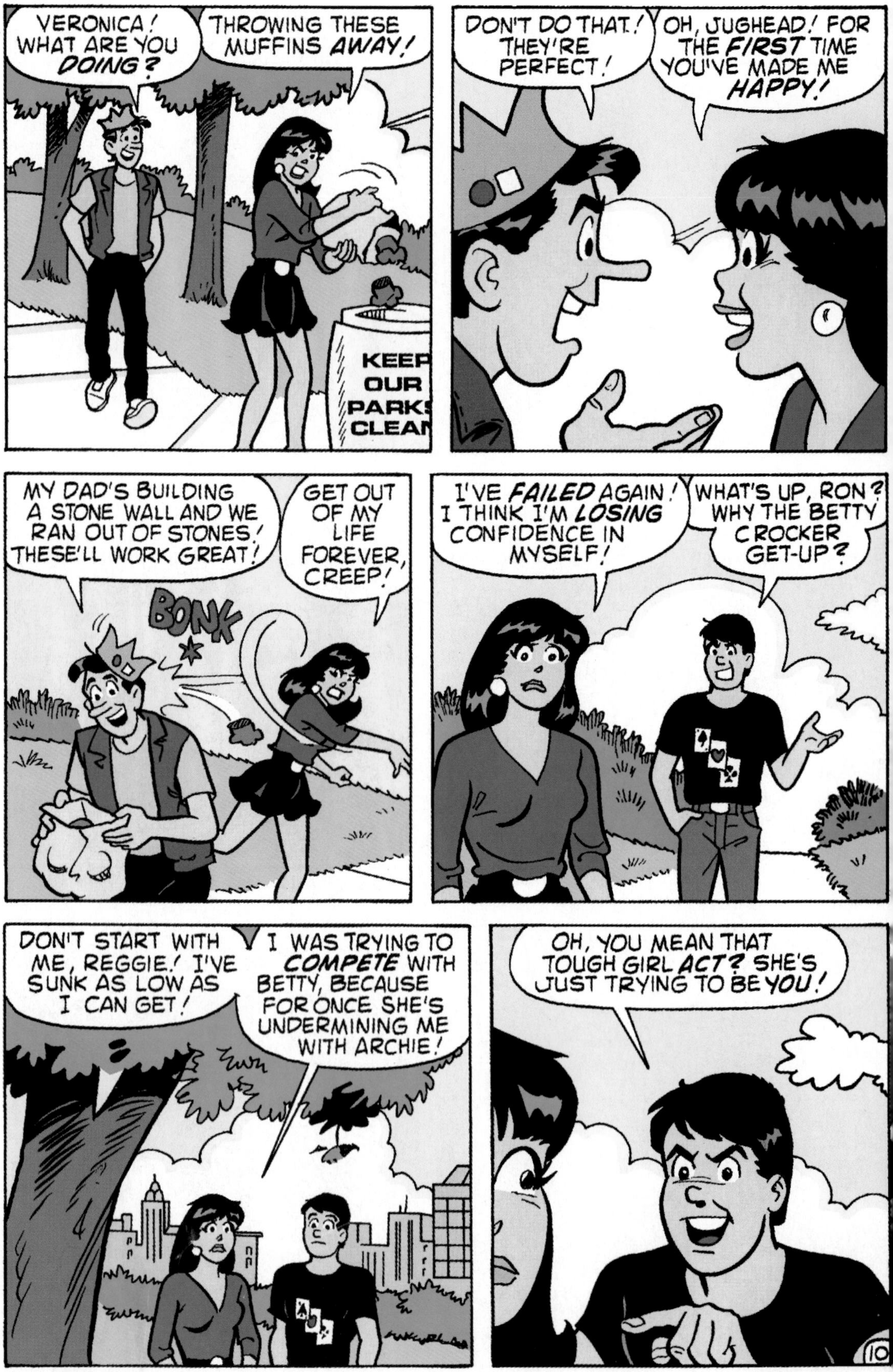
VERONICA! WHAT ARE YOU DOING?
THROWING THESE MUFFINS AWAY!
KEEP OUR PARKS CLEAN
DON'T DO THAT! THEY'RE PERFECT!
OH, JUGHEAD! FOR THE FIRST TIME YOU'VE MADE ME HAPPY!
MY DAD'S BUILDING A STONE WALL AND WE RAN OUT OF STONES! THESE'LL WORK GREAT!
GET OUT OF MY LIFE FOREVER, CREEP!
BONK
I'VE FAILED AGAIN! I THINK I'M LOSING CONFIDENCE IN MYSELF!
WHAT'S UP, RON? WHY THE BETTY CROCKER GET-UP?
DON'T START WITH ME, REGGIE! I'VE SUNK AS LOW AS I CAN GET!
I WAS TRYING TO COMPETE WITH BETTY, BECAUSE FOR ONCE SHE'S UNDERMINING ME WITH ARCHIE!
OH, YOU MEAN THAT TOUGH GIRL ACT? SHE'S JUST TRYING TO BE YOU!
10

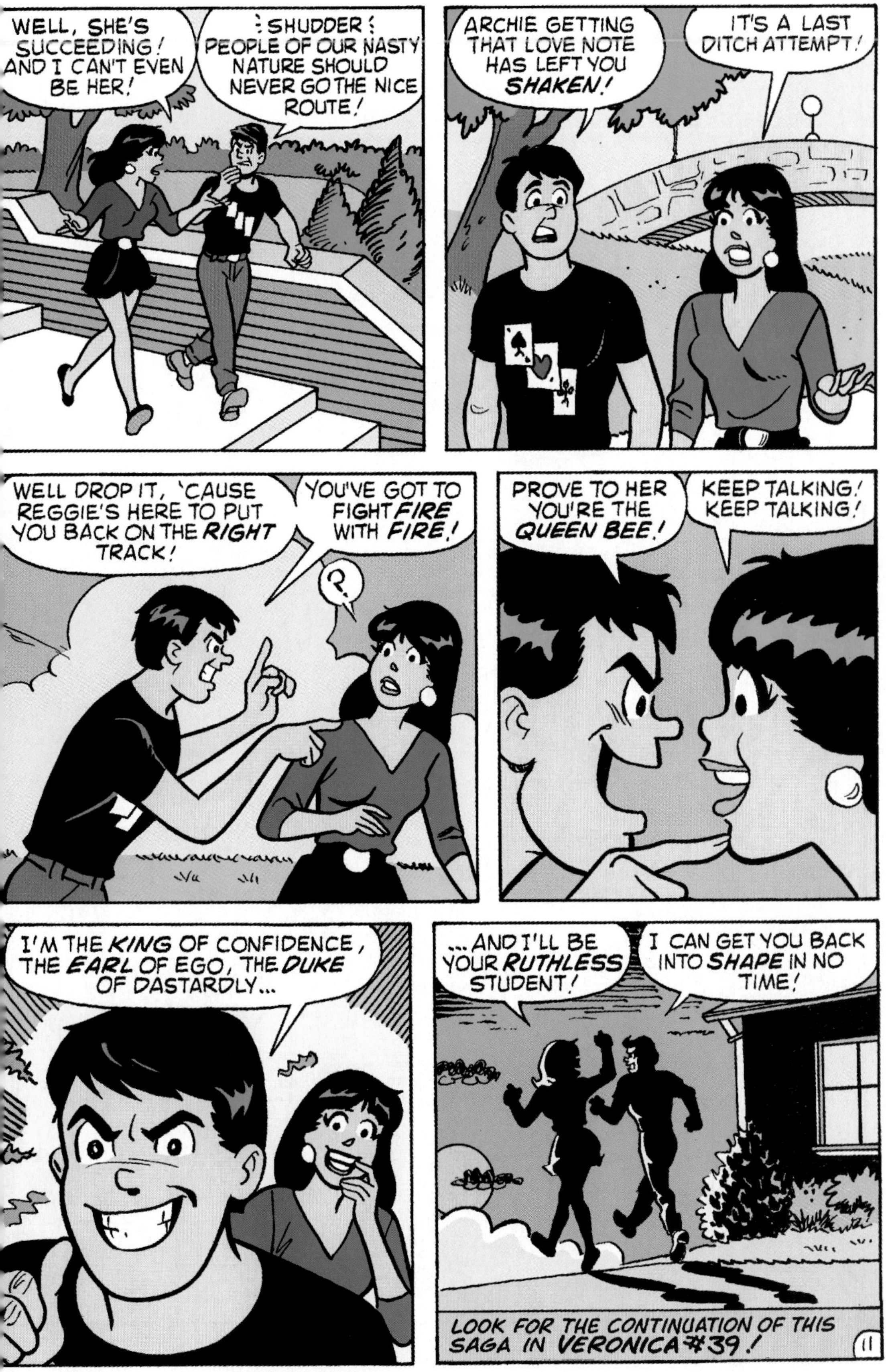

WELL, SHE'S SUCCEEDING! AND I CAN'T EVEN BE HER!
SHUDDER PEOPLE OF OUR NASTY NATURE SHOULD NEVER GO THE NICE ROUTE!
ARCHIE GETTING THAT LOVE NOTE HAS LEFT YOU SHAKEN!
IT'S A LAST DITCH ATTEMPT!
WELL DROP IT, 'CAUSE REGGIE'S HERE TO PUT YOU BACK ON THE RIGHT TRACK!
YOU'VE GOT TO FIGHT FIRE WITH FIRE!
?
PROVE TO HER YOU'RE THE QUEEN BEE!
KEEP TALKING! KEEP TALKING!
I'M THE KING OF CONFIDENCE, THE EARL OF EGO, THE DUKE OF DASTARDLY...
...AND I'LL BE YOUR RUTHLESS STUDENT!
I CAN GET YOU BACK INTO SHAPE IN NO TIME!
LOOK FOR THE CONTINUATION OF THIS SAGA IN VERONICA #39!
11

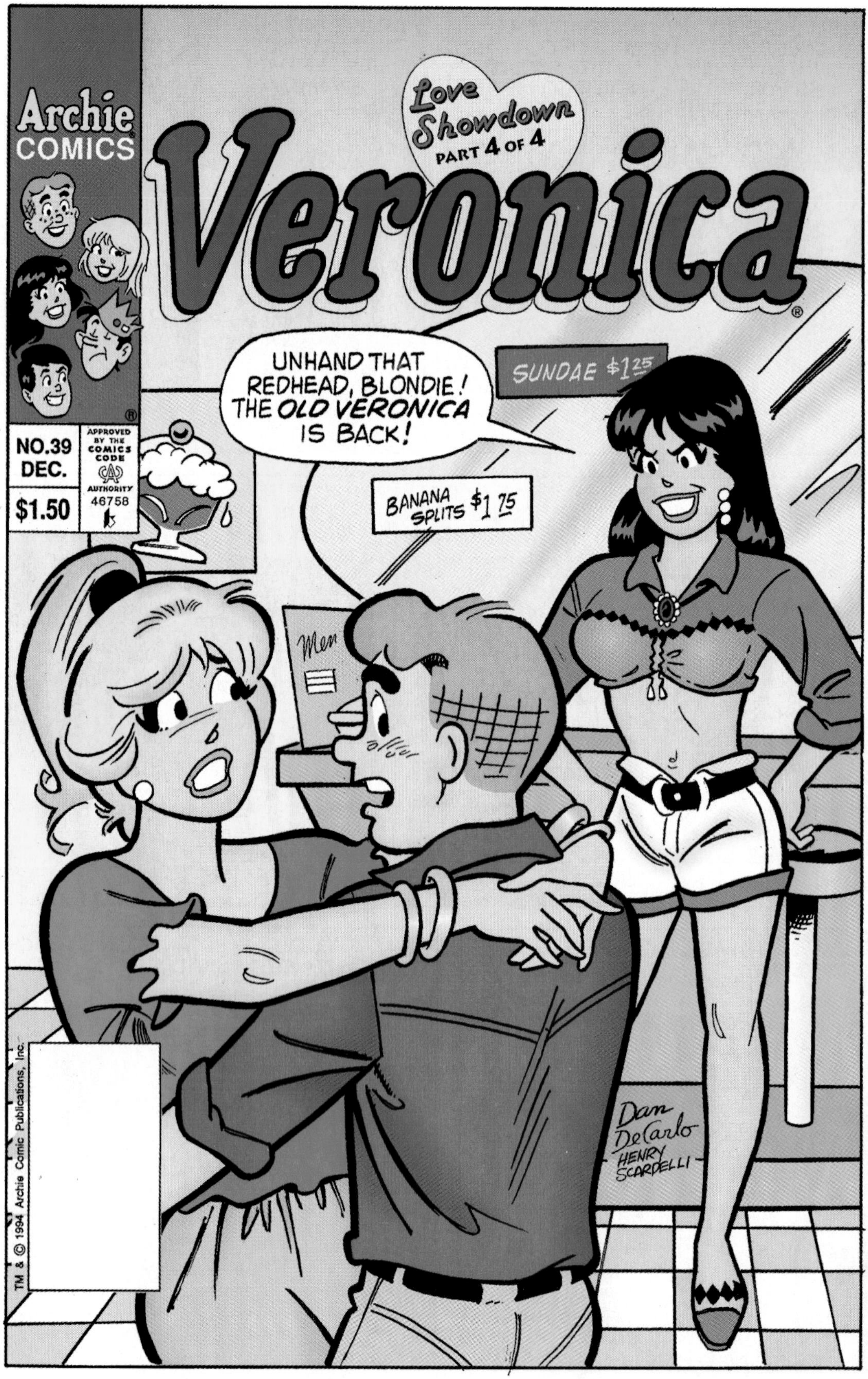
Archie COMICS
Love Showdown PART 4 OF 4
Veronica
NO.39 DEC.
$1.50
APPROVED BY THE COMICS CODE AUTHORITY
UNHAND THAT REDHEAD, BLONDIE! THE OLD VERONICA IS BACK!
SUNDAE $1.25
BANANA SPLITS $1.75
Dan DeCarlo
HENRY SCARPELLI
TM & © 1994 Archie Comic Publications, Inc.

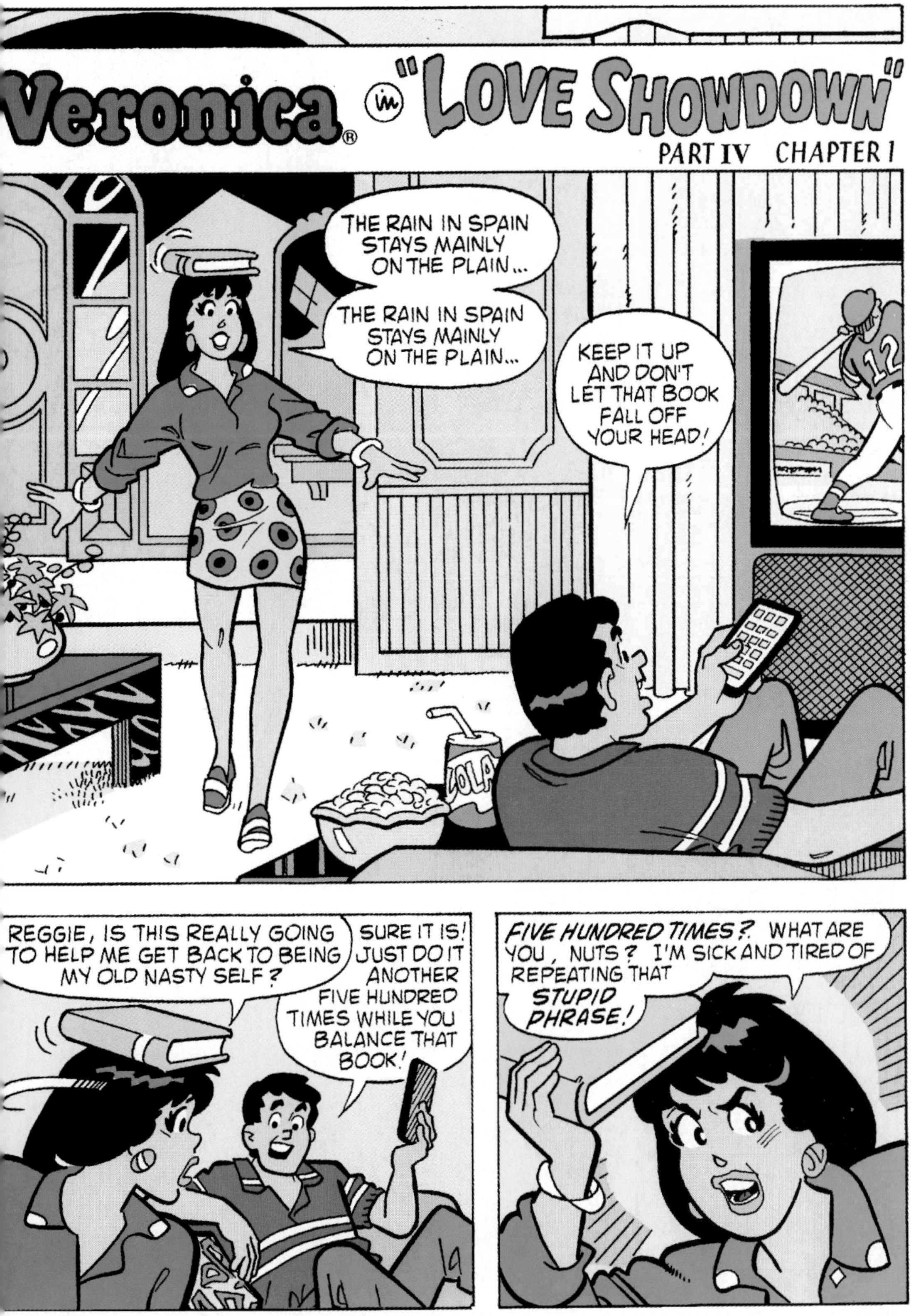
Veronica® in "LOVE SHOWDOWN"
PART IV CHAPTER 1
THE RAIN IN SPAIN STAYS MAINLY ON THE PLAIN...
THE RAIN IN SPAIN STAYS MAINLY ON THE PLAIN...
KEEP IT UP AND DON'T LET THAT BOOK FALL OFF YOUR HEAD!
12
COLA
REGGIE, IS THIS REALLY GOING TO HELP ME GET BACK TO BEING MY OLD NASTY SELF?
SURE IT IS! JUST DO IT ANOTHER FIVE HUNDRED TIMES WHILE YOU BALANCE THAT BOOK!
FIVE HUNDRED TIMES? WHAT ARE YOU, NUTS? I'M SICK AND TIRED OF REPEATING THAT STUPID PHRASE!

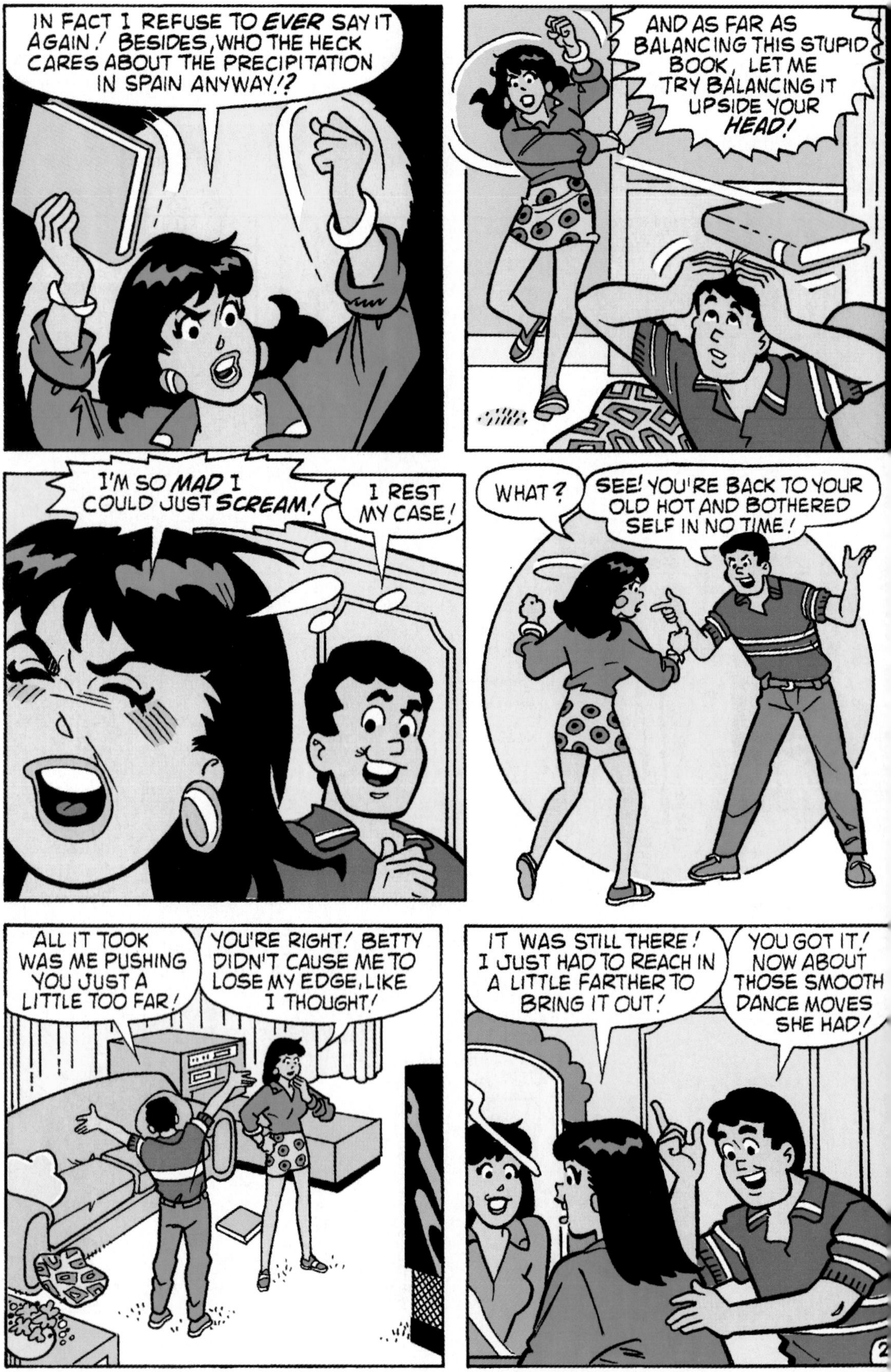
IN FACT I REFUSE TO EVER SAY IT AGAIN! BESIDES, WHO THE HECK CARES ABOUT THE PRECIPITATION IN SPAIN ANYWAY!?
AND AS FAR AS BALANCING THIS STUPID BOOK, LET ME TRY BALANCING IT UPSIDE YOUR HEAD!
I'M SO MAD I COULD JUST SCREAM!
I REST MY CASE!
WHAT?
SEE! YOU'RE BACK TO YOUR OLD HOT AND BOTHERED SELF IN NO TIME!
ALL IT TOOK WAS ME PUSHING YOU JUST A LITTLE TOO FAR!
YOU'RE RIGHT! BETTY DIDN'T CAUSE ME TO LOSE MY EDGE, LIKE I THOUGHT!
IT WAS STILL THERE! I JUST HAD TO REACH IN A LITTLE FARTHER TO BRING IT OUT!
YOU GOT IT! NOW ABOUT THOSE SMOOTH DANCE MOVES SHE HAD!

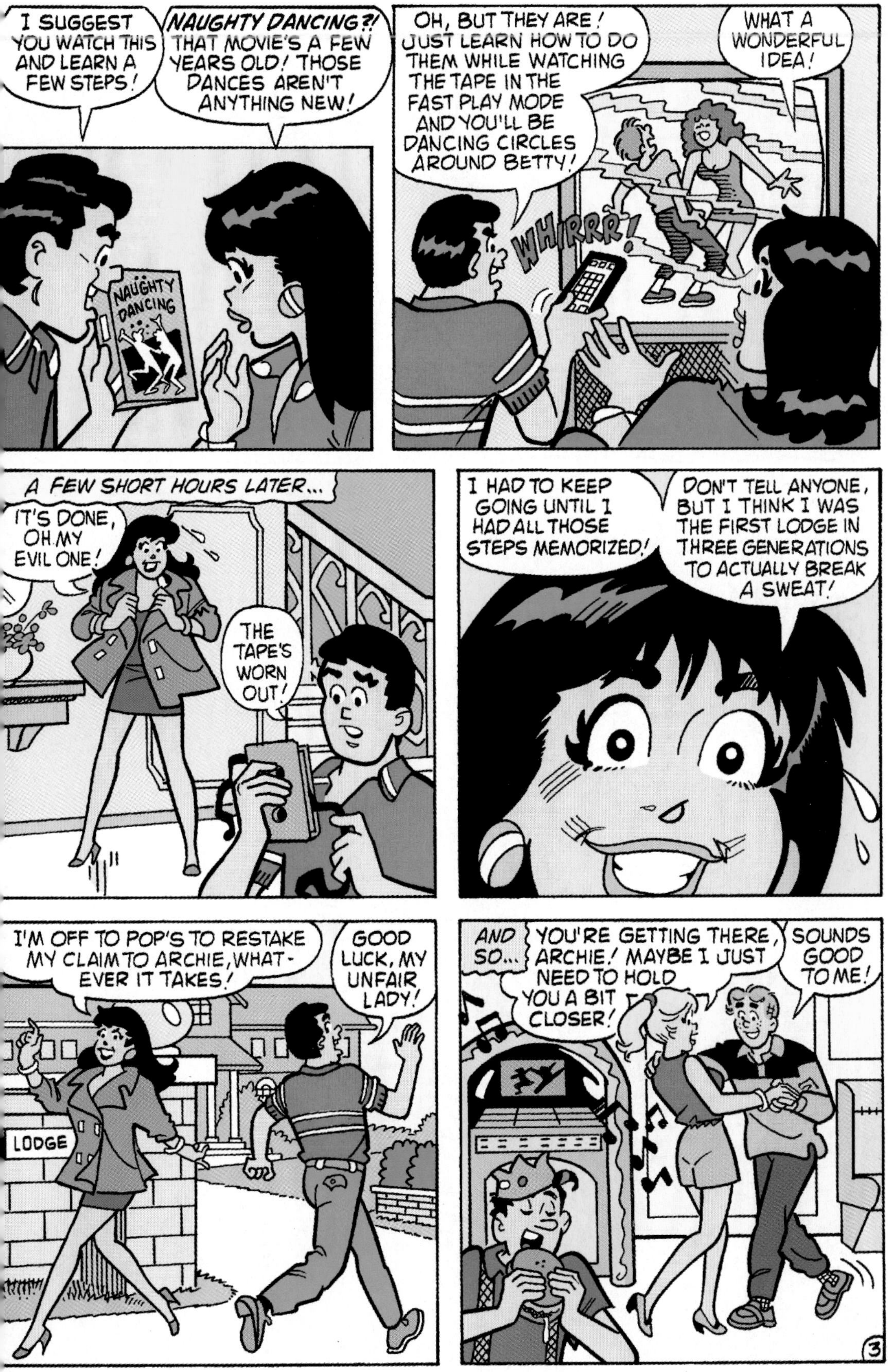
I SUGGEST YOU WATCH THIS AND LEARN A FEW STEPS!
NAUGHTY DANCING?! THAT MOVIE'S A FEW YEARS OLD! THOSE DANCES AREN'T ANYTHING NEW!
NAUGHTY DANCING
OH, BUT THEY ARE! JUST LEARN HOW TO DO THEM WHILE WATCHING THE TAPE IN THE FAST PLAY MODE AND YOU'LL BE DANCING CIRCLES AROUND BETTY!
WHAT A WONDERFUL IDEA!
WHIRRR!
A FEW SHORT HOURS LATER...
IT'S DONE, OH MY EVIL ONE!
THE TAPE'S WORN OUT!
I HAD TO KEEP GOING UNTIL I HAD ALL THOSE STEPS MEMORIZED!
DON'T TELL ANYONE, BUT I THINK I WAS THE FIRST LODGE IN THREE GENERATIONS TO ACTUALLY BREAK A SWEAT!
I'M OFF TO POP'S TO RESTAKE MY CLAIM TO ARCHIE, WHAT-EVER IT TAKES!
GOOD LUCK, MY UNFAIR LADY!
LODGE
AND SO...
YOU'RE GETTING THERE, ARCHIE! MAYBE I JUST NEED TO HOLD YOU A BIT CLOSER!
SOUNDS GOOD TO ME!
3

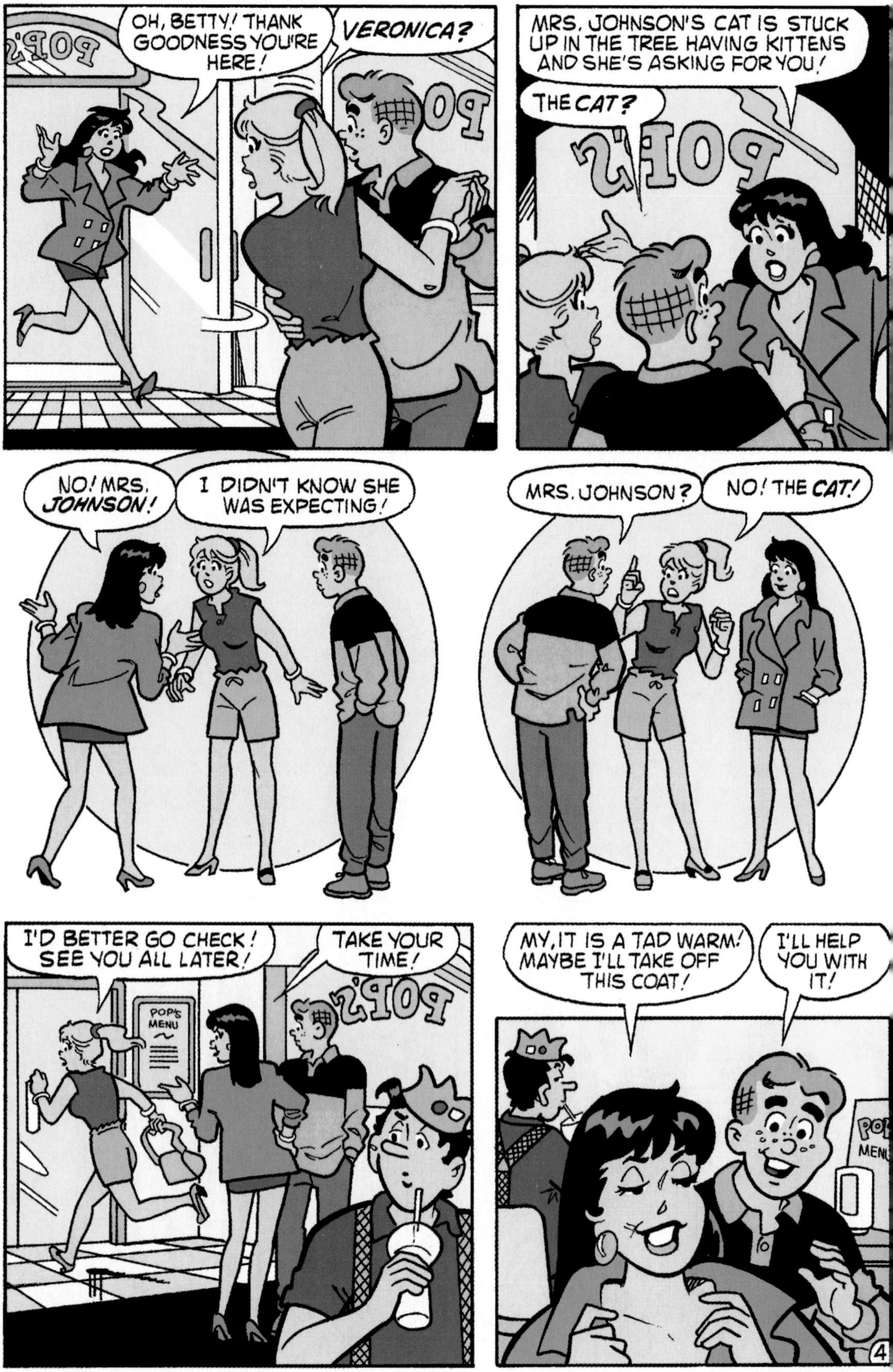
OH, BETTY! THANK GOODNESS YOU'RE HERE!
VERONICA?
MRS. JOHNSON'S CAT IS STUCK UP IN THE TREE HAVING KITTENS AND SHE'S ASKING FOR YOU!
THE CAT?
POP'S
NO! MRS. JOHNSON!
I DIDN'T KNOW SHE WAS EXPECTING!
MRS. JOHNSON?
NO! THE CAT!
I'D BETTER GO CHECK! SEE YOU ALL LATER!
TAKE YOUR TIME!
POP'S MENU
MY, IT IS A TAD WARM! MAYBE I'LL TAKE OFF THIS COAT!
I'LL HELP YOU WITH IT!

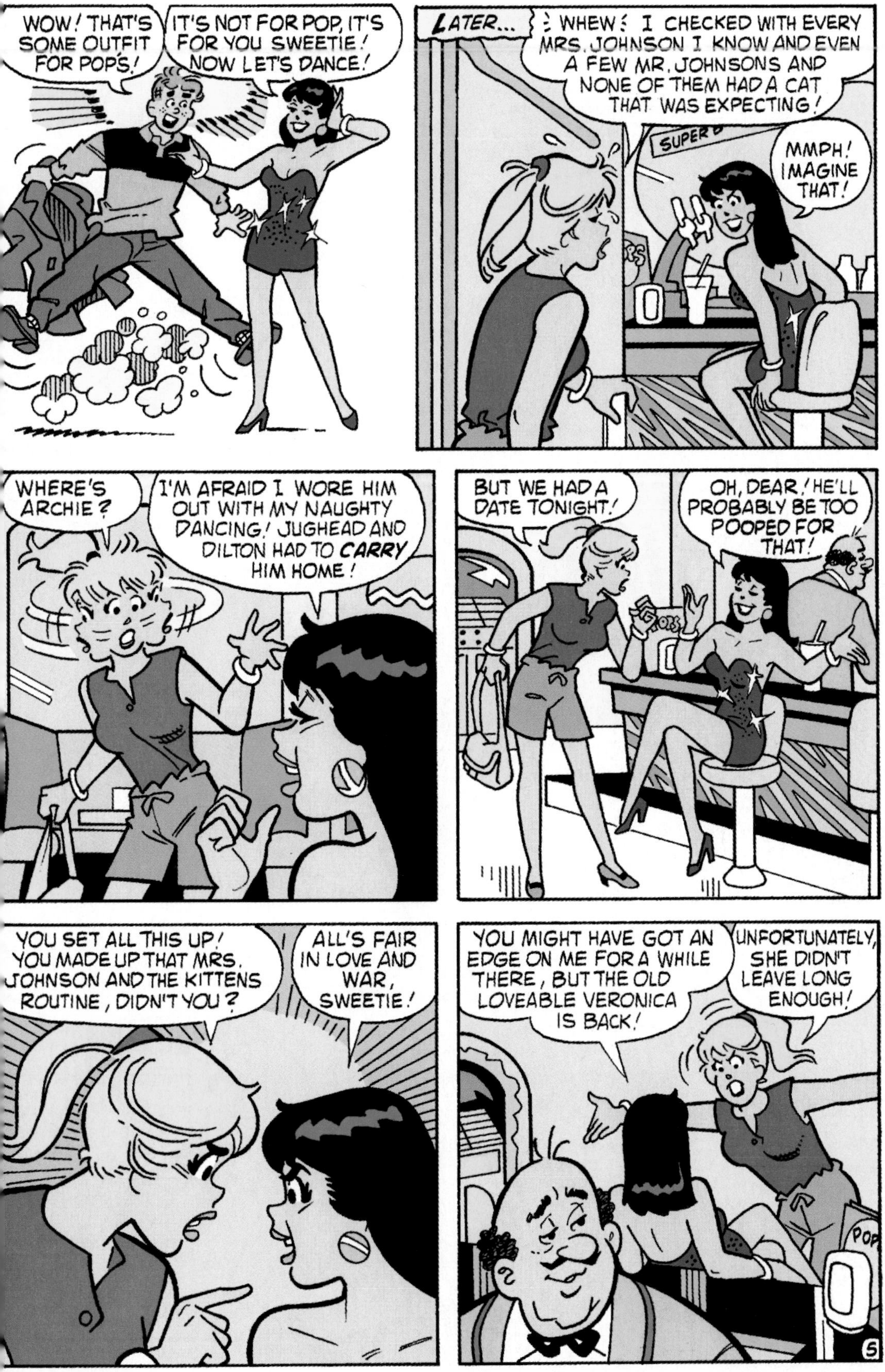
WOW! THAT'S SOME OUTFIT FOR POP'S!
IT'S NOT FOR POP, IT'S FOR YOU SWEETIE! NOW LET'S DANCE!
LATER...
WHEW! I CHECKED WITH EVERY MRS. JOHNSON I KNOW AND EVEN A FEW MR. JOHNSONS AND NONE OF THEM HAD A CAT THAT WAS EXPECTING!
SUPER
MMPH! IMAGINE THAT!
WHERE'S ARCHIE?
I'M AFRAID I WORE HIM OUT WITH MY NAUGHTY DANCING! JUGHEAD AND DILTON HAD TO CARRY HIM HOME!
BUT WE HAD A DATE TONIGHT!
OH, DEAR! HE'LL PROBABLY BE TOO POOPED FOR THAT!
POPS
YOU SET ALL THIS UP! YOU MADE UP THAT MRS. JOHNSON AND THE KITTENS ROUTINE, DIDN'T YOU?
ALL'S FAIR IN LOVE AND WAR, SWEETIE!
YOU MIGHT HAVE GOT AN EDGE ON ME FOR A WHILE THERE, BUT THE OLD LOVEABLE VERONICA IS BACK!
UNFORTUNATELY, SHE DIDN'T LEAVE LONG ENOUGH!
POP
5

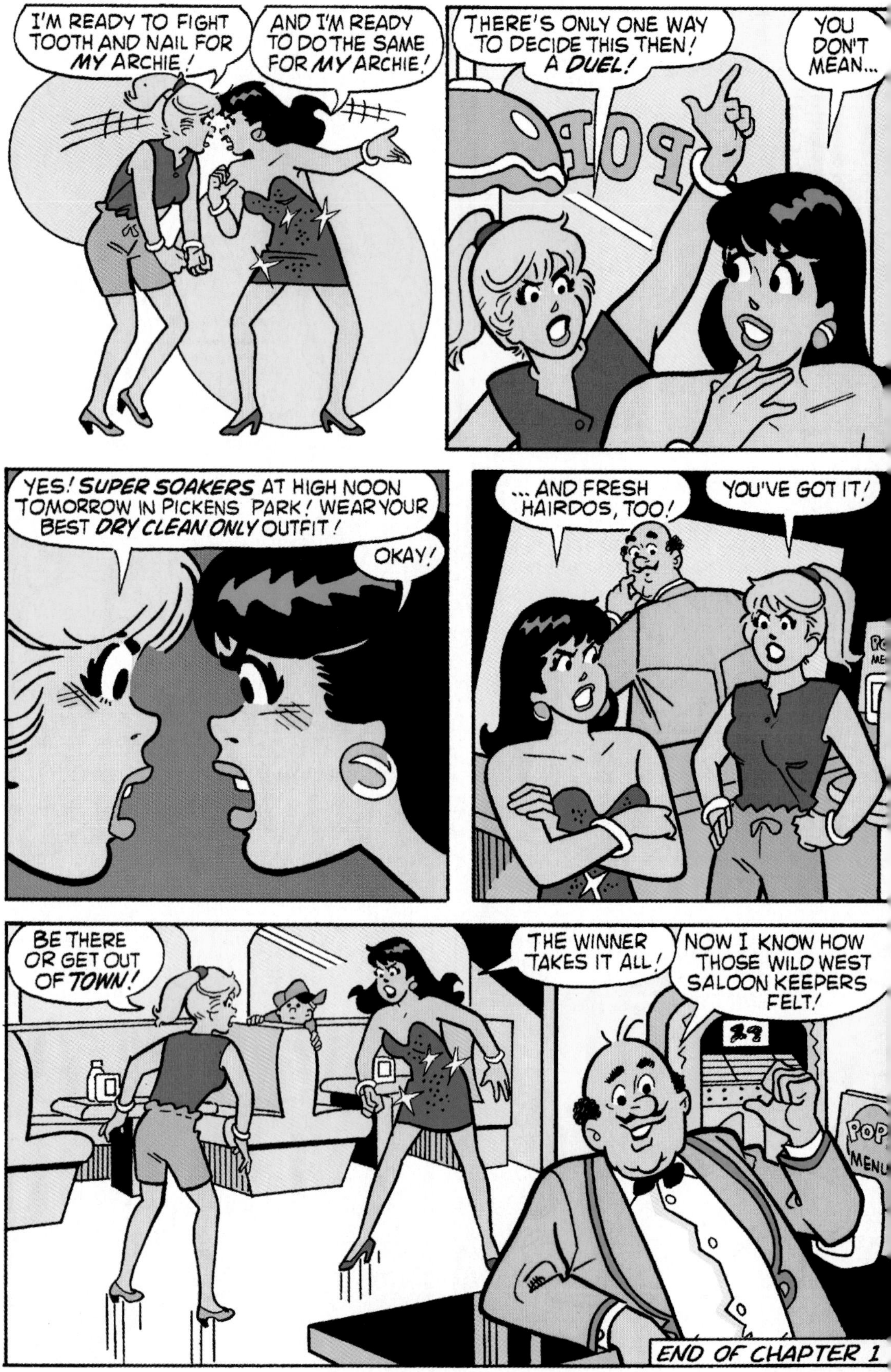
I'M READY TO FIGHT TOOTH AND NAIL FOR MY ARCHIE!
AND I'M READY TO DO THE SAME FOR MY ARCHIE!
THERE'S ONLY ONE WAY TO DECIDE THIS THEN! A DUEL!
YOU DON'T MEAN...
POP
YES! SUPER SOAKERS AT HIGH NOON TOMORROW IN PICKENS PARK! WEAR YOUR BEST DRY CLEAN ONLY OUTFIT!
OKAY!
...AND FRESH HAIRDOS, TOO!
YOU'VE GOT IT!
BE THERE OR GET OUT OF TOWN!
THE WINNER TAKES IT ALL!
NOW I KNOW HOW THOSE WILD WEST SALOON KEEPERS FELT!
END OF CHAPTER 1

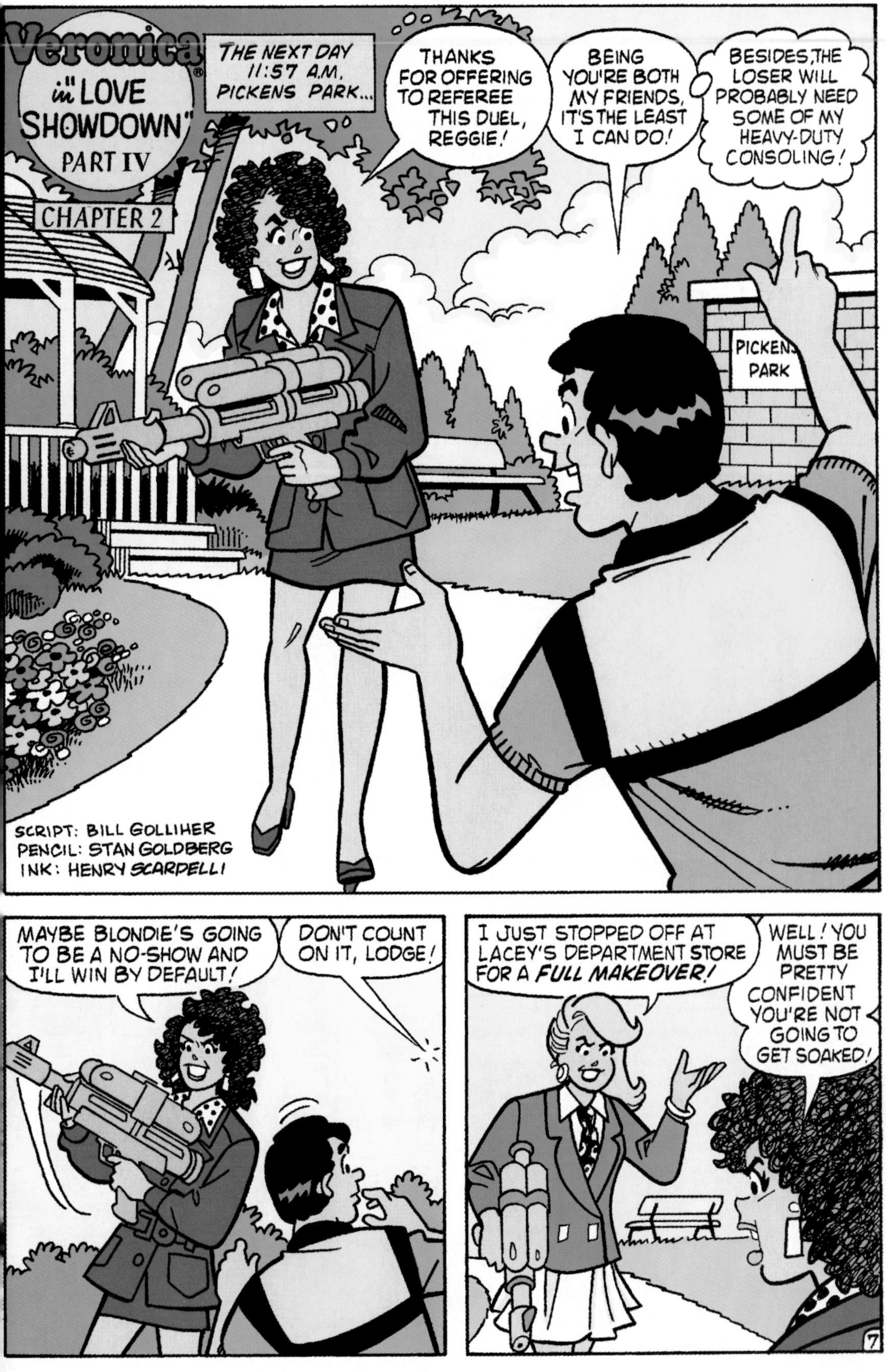

Veronica®
in "LOVE SHOWDOWN" PART IV
CHAPTER 2
THE NEXT DAY 11:57 A.M. PICKENS PARK...
THANKS FOR OFFERING TO REFEREE THIS DUEL, REGGIE!
BEING YOU'RE BOTH MY FRIENDS, IT'S THE LEAST I CAN DO!
BESIDES, THE LOSER WILL PROBABLY NEED SOME OF MY HEAVY-DUTY CONSOLING!
PICKENS PARK
SCRIPT: BILL GOLLIHER
PENCIL: STAN GOLDBERG
INK: HENRY SCARPELLI
MAYBE BLONDIE'S GOING TO BE A NO-SHOW AND I'LL WIN BY DEFAULT!
DON'T COUNT ON IT, LODGE!
I JUST STOPPED OFF AT LACEY'S DEPARTMENT STORE FOR A FULL MAKEOVER!
WELL! YOU MUST BE PRETTY CONFIDENT YOU'RE NOT GOING TO GET SOAKED!
7

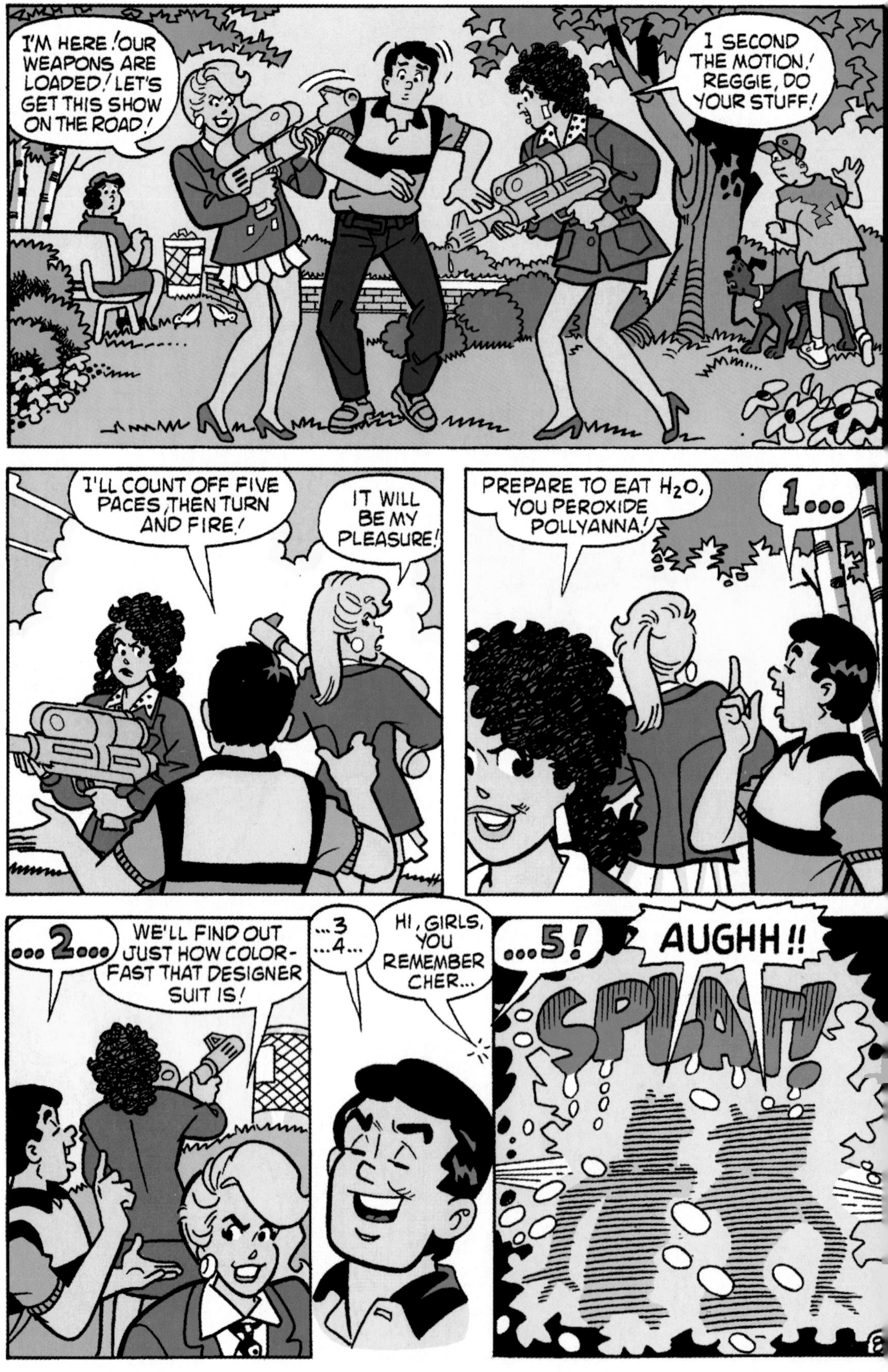
I'M HERE! OUR WEAPONS ARE LOADED! LET'S GET THIS SHOW ON THE ROAD!
I SECOND THE MOTION! REGGIE, DO YOUR STUFF!
I'LL COUNT OFF FIVE PACES, THEN TURN AND FIRE!
IT WILL BE MY PLEASURE!
PREPARE TO EAT H_2O, YOU PEROXIDE POLLYANNA!
1...
...2...
WE'LL FIND OUT JUST HOW COLOR-FAST THAT DESIGNER SUIT IS!
...3 ...4...
HI, GIRLS, YOU REMEMBER CHER...
...5!
AUGHH!!
SPLAT!

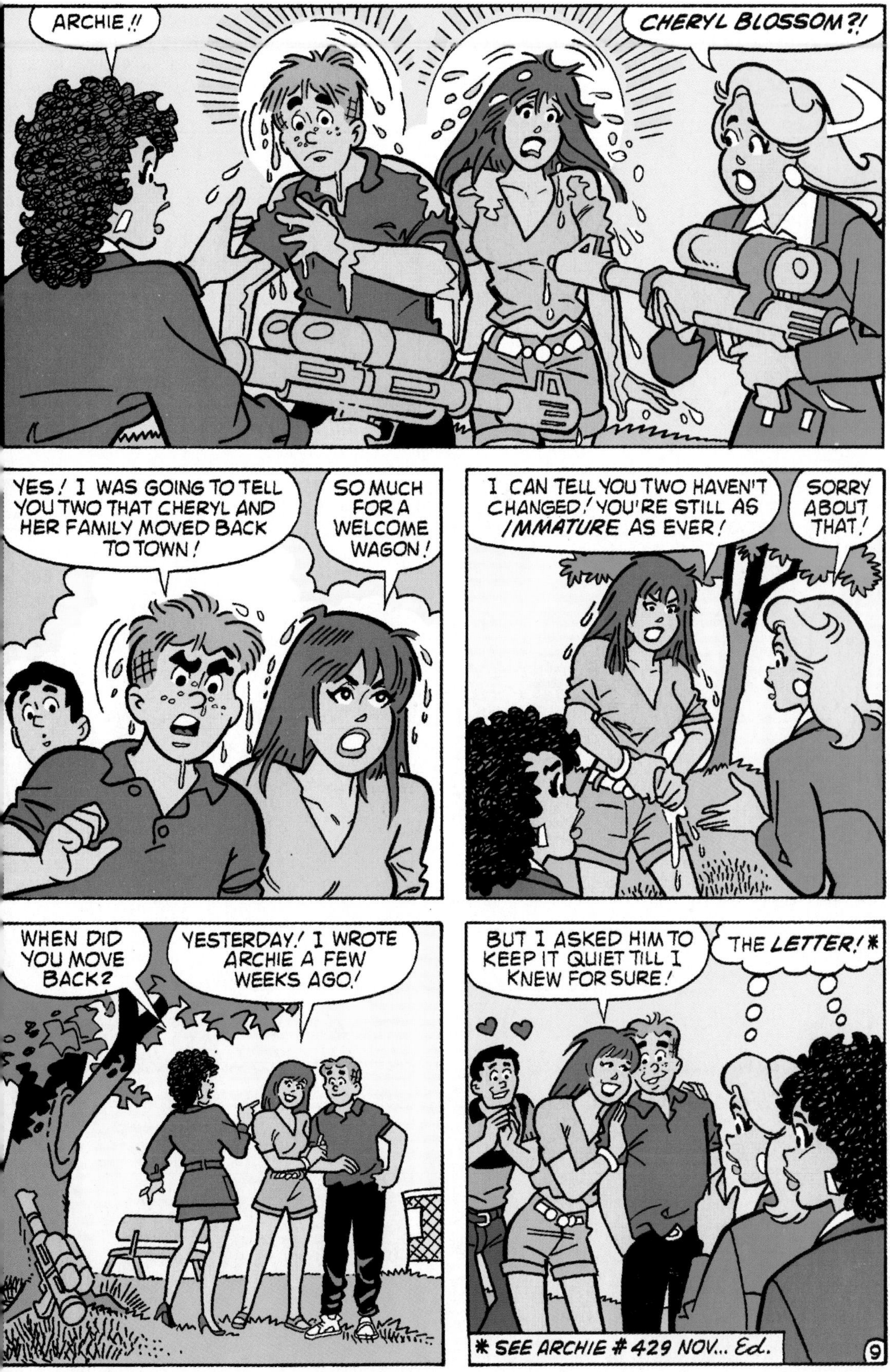
ARCHIE?!!
CHERYL BLOSSOM?!
YES! I WAS GOING TO TELL YOU TWO THAT CHERYL AND HER FAMILY MOVED BACK TO TOWN!
SO MUCH FOR A WELCOME WAGON!
I CAN TELL YOU TWO HAVEN'T CHANGED! YOU'RE STILL AS IMMATURE AS EVER!
SORRY ABOUT THAT!
WHEN DID YOU MOVE BACK?
YESTERDAY! I WROTE ARCHIE A FEW WEEKS AGO!
BUT I ASKED HIM TO KEEP IT QUIET TILL I KNEW FOR SURE!
THE LETTER! *
* SEE ARCHIE # 429 NOV... Ed.

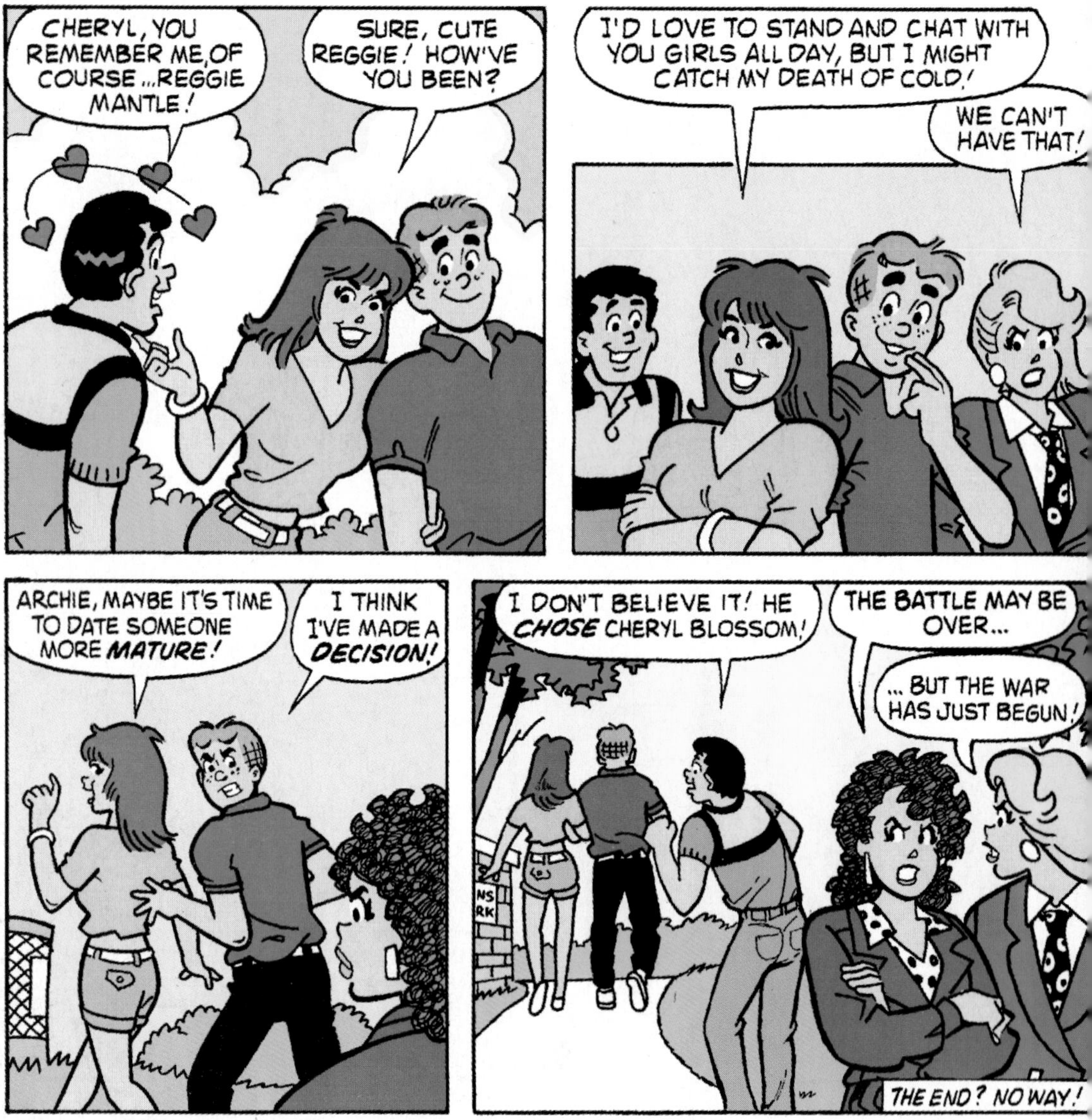
CHERYL, YOU REMEMBER ME, OF COURSE ...REGGIE MANTLE!
SURE, CUTE REGGIE! HOW'VE YOU BEEN?
I'D LOVE TO STAND AND CHAT WITH YOU GIRLS ALL DAY, BUT I MIGHT CATCH MY DEATH OF COLD!
WE CAN'T HAVE THAT!
ARCHIE, MAYBE IT'S TIME TO DATE SOMEONE MORE MATURE!
I THINK I'VE MADE A DECISION!
I DON'T BELIEVE IT! HE CHOSE CHERYL BLOSSOM!
THE BATTLE MAY BE OVER...
... BUT THE WAR HAS JUST BEGUN!
THE END? NO WAY!

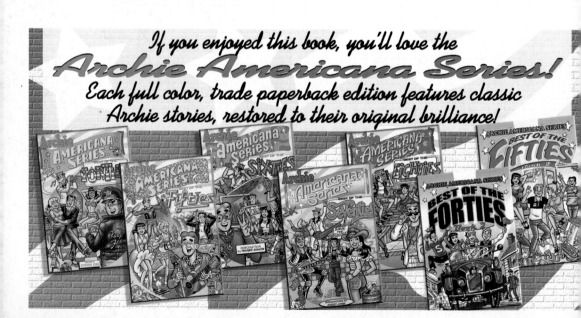